Teacher Guide

Passwords

Social Studies Vocabulary

Developer: Maureen Devine Sotoohi

Writers: Laura Johnson and Barbara Fierman

Cover Design: Susan Hawk

Photo Credits: Front cover: clockwise from top left: Suzanne Tucker/Shutterstock.com; Tim McCabe/USDA; PhotoLiz/Shutterstock.com; Lynn Watson/Shutterstock.com

Reviewers: Curriculum Associates, Inc. would like to acknowledge the contribution of the educators who reviewed ***Passwords*** at various stages of its development. Their insightful comments have made our program a better one for teachers and students.

Gracie Alvear
Bilingual/ESL/Immigrant Student Service
Elementary Supervisor
Edinburg CISD
Edinburg, Texas

Jackie Baldwin
Secondary Reading Senior Coordinator
Instructional Services Division
Polk County Schools
Bartow, Florida

Lorraine Cruz
Principal
Ames Middle School
Chicago, Illinois

Leonila Izaguirre
Bilingual-ESL Director
Pharr-San Juan-Alamo ISD
Pharr, Texas

Judy Lewis
Director, State and Federal Programs
Folsom Cordova Unified School District
Folsom, California

Dominique Mongeau
Categorical Program Adviser
Carson Street Elementary School
Los Angeles Unified School District
Carson, California

CURRICULUM ASSOCIATES®, INC.

Table of Contents

ISBN 978-0-7609-4499-8

15 14 13 12 11 10 9 8 7 6 5 4 3 2 1

Overview

Passwords: Social Studies Vocabulary is designed to build the vocabulary essential to understanding the key concepts students are studying in social studies. The topic areas and vocabulary words used in ***Passwords: Social Studies Vocabulary*** have been chosen based on state social studies standards. The topics and vocabulary words also align with the basal social studies textbooks of major publishers.

Passwords: Social Studies Vocabulary is recommended for all students who need practice with the vocabulary that will help them succeed in social studies. These students may include English language learners as well as other striving learners. See pages 11–13 of this teacher guide for vocabulary teaching strategies that will help teachers meet the needs of all their students.

The lessons in ***Passwords: Social Studies Vocabulary*** may be taught in the order presented in the book or in another sequence that aligns with your social studies curriculum. Teachers may choose to go through the book lesson by lesson. Alternatively, teachers may use only the lessons that correspond to the social studies topic being taught in class. By providing an overview of grade-appropriate topics, ***Passwords: Social Studies Vocabulary*** may also be used to help students prepare and review for standardized tests in social studies.

The ***Passwords: Social Studies Vocabulary*** student book reading passages are available on an audio CD. The CD is a useful tool to use with English language learners or other students who would benefit from listening to the reading passage multiple times. Auditory learners will find listening to the passages on the CD especially helpful.

Student Books

Passwords: Social Studies Vocabulary student books have been written and designed to provide students with a text that is "considerate," or reader friendly. Three hallmarks of considerate text are: clear text structure, coherent writing, and audience appropriateness. ***Passwords: Social Studies Vocabulary*** incorporates these characteristics of considerate text into every lesson.

Text Structure
The reading selections in ***Passwords: Social Studies Vocabulary*** feature text structures that exhibit clear organizational patterns. In descriptive text, information is given in a logical order of importance. For sequential text, events are presented in the order in which they occur. In cause-and-effect text, the relation between the actions or events is clearly stated.

Coherent Writing
The concepts and ideas presented in ***Passwords: Social Studies Vocabulary*** are clearly stated. An introductory paragraph states the topic of the lesson. All the information in the reading selection connects to the topic. No extraneous material confuses readers. Headings and subheads highlight the cohesion of each text segment. Transitional words and phrases signal the relation between actions or concepts.

Audience Appropriateness
Although the readability of ***Passwords: Social Studies Vocabulary*** reading passages is below grade level, the concepts and material in the passages are grade appropriate. Prereading activities activate students' prior knowledge. Activities that follow the reading passage help teachers evaluate student understanding.

Look for these signs of considerate text in the ***Passwords: Social Studies Vocabulary*** student books.

- Short line length for increased readability
- Simple sentence structure
- Paragraphs with clear topic sentences and relevant supporting details
- Introductory subheads
- Vocabulary words boldfaced in text
- Definitions of vocabulary words near the first use of the word
- Simple font
- Clean page layout
- Appropriate, not overwhelming, visuals
- Illustrations support content

The student book for Book B has 12 lessons. Each lesson introduces and practices eight key vocabulary words related to a single social studies topic.

Features of the Lesson

Each lesson of the student book contains these features:

- Target Vocabulary
- Lesson Opener
- Reading Passage
- Graphics
- Activities A–C
- Word Fun
- Write!

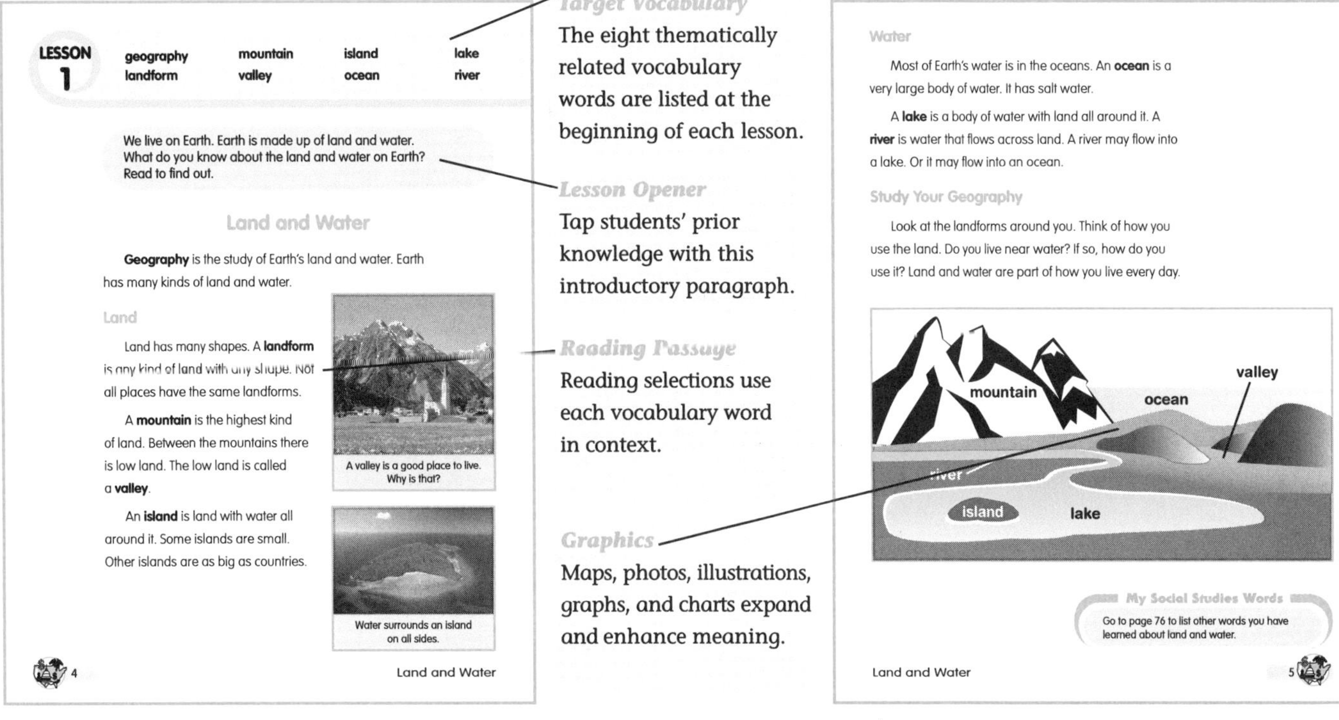

LESSON 1

geography	mountain	island	lake
landform	valley	ocean	river

We live on Earth. Earth is made up of land and water. What do you know about the land and water on Earth? Read to find out.

Land and Water

Geography is the study of Earth's land and water. Earth has many kinds of land and water.

Land

Land has many shapes. A **landform** is any kind of land with any shape. Not all places have the same landforms.

A **mountain** is the highest kind of land. Between the mountains there is low land. The low land is called a **valley**.

An **island** is land with water all around it. Some islands are small. Other islands are as big as countries.

A valley is a good place to live. Why is that?

Water surrounds an island on all sides.

4 Land and Water

Target Vocabulary
The eight thematically related vocabulary words are listed at the beginning of each lesson.

Lesson Opener
Tap students' prior knowledge with this introductory paragraph.

Reading Passage
Reading selections use each vocabulary word in context.

Graphics
Maps, photos, illustrations, graphs, and charts expand and enhance meaning.

Water

Most of Earth's water is in the oceans. An **ocean** is a very large body of water. It has salt water.

A **lake** is a body of water with land all around it. A **river** is water that flows across land. A river may flow into a lake. Or it may flow into an ocean.

Study Your Geography

Look at the landforms around you. Think of how you use the land. Do you live near water? If so, how do you use it? Land and water are part of how you live every day.

My Social Studies Words
Go to page 76 to list other words you have learned about land and water.

Land and Water 5

Progressively difficult activities follow each reading passage.

Activity A

Students match vocabulary words with pictures or draw pictures that show their understanding of the words.

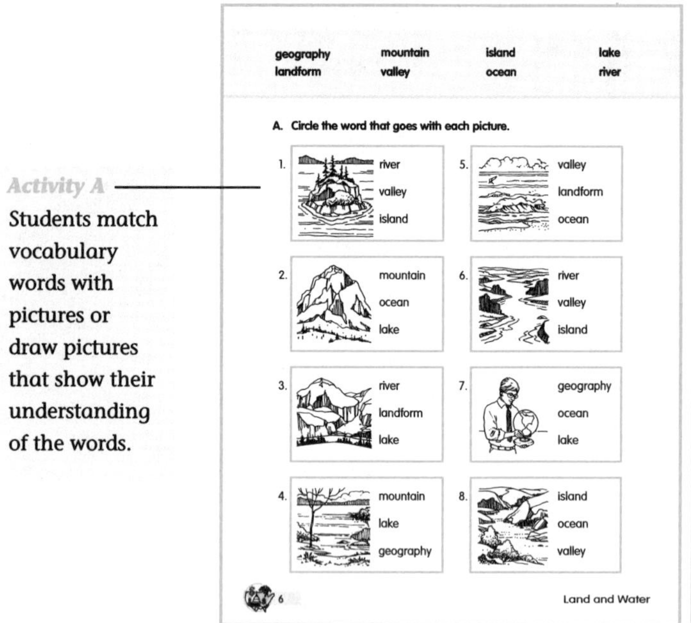

geography **mountain** **island** **lake**
landform **valley** **ocean** **river**

A. Circle the word that goes with each picture.

1. river / valley / island
2. mountain / ocean / lake
3. river / landform / lake
4. mountain / lake / geography
5. valley / landform / ocean
6. river / valley / island
7. geography / ocean / lake
8. island / ocean / valley

6 Land and Water

Activity B

Students choose the vocabulary word that correctly answers a riddle or match a word to its definition.

Word Fun

Students learn more about a target vocabulary word.

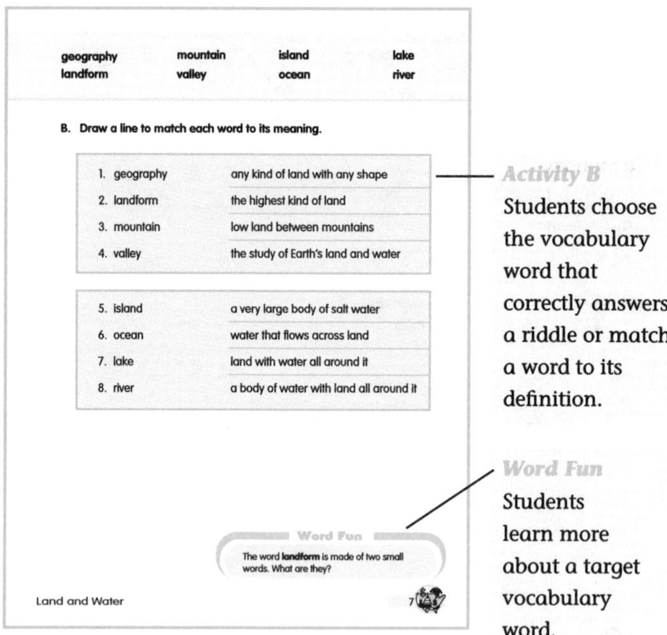

geography **mountain** **island** **lake**
landform **valley** **ocean** **river**

B. Draw a line to match each word to its meaning.

1. geography	any kind of land with any shape
2. landform	the highest kind of land
3. mountain	low land between mountains
4. valley	the study of Earth's land and water

5. island	a very large body of salt water
6. ocean	water that flows across land
7. lake	land with water all around it
8. river	a body of water with land all around it

Word Fun

The word **landform** is made of two small words. What are they?

Land and Water 7

Activity C

Students use vocabulary words in cloze sentences.

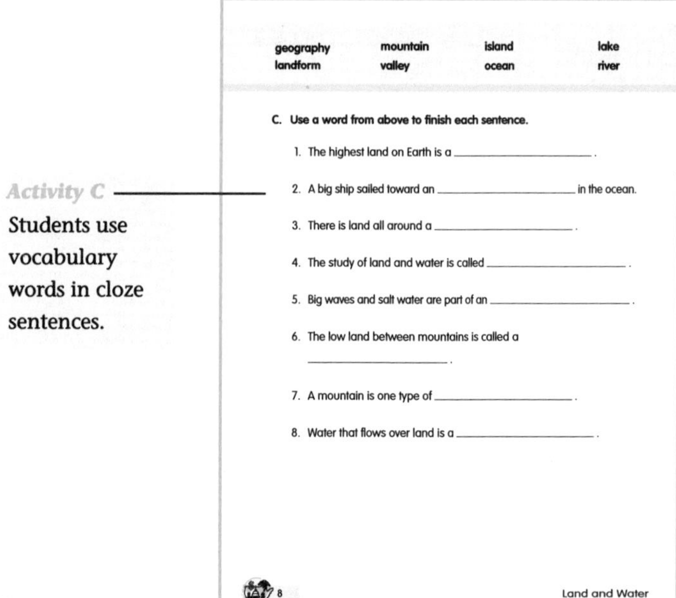

geography **mountain** **island** **lake**
landform **valley** **ocean** **river**

C. Use a word from above to finish each sentence.

1. The highest land on Earth is a ______________.
2. A big ship sailed toward an ______________ in the ocean.
3. There is land all around a ______________.
4. The study of land and water is called ______________.
5. Big waves and salt water are part of an ______________.
6. The low land between mountains is called a ______________.
7. A mountain is one type of ______________.
8. Water that flows over land is a ______________.

8 Land and Water

Write!

An independent writing activity strengthens and expands students' experience with the vocabulary.

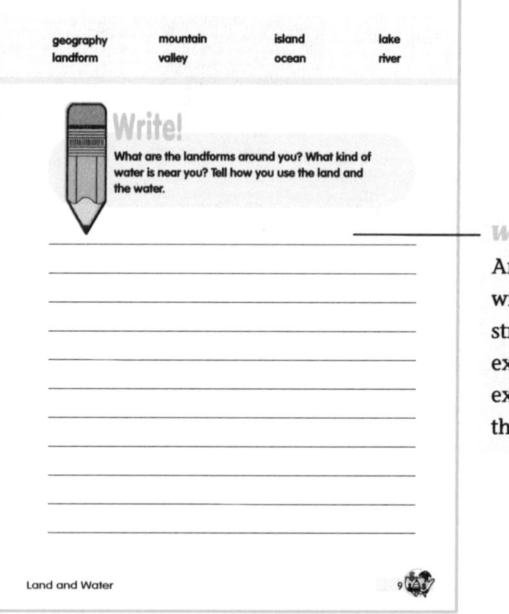

geography **mountain** **island** **lake**
landform **valley** **ocean** **river**

Write!

What are the landforms around you? What kind of water is near you? Tell how you use the land and the water.

Land and Water 9

My Social Studies Words

Students create a personal dictionary organized by topic area.

My Social Studies Words

Lesson 1 Land and Water	Lesson 2 Communities Are Different

76 My Social Studies Words

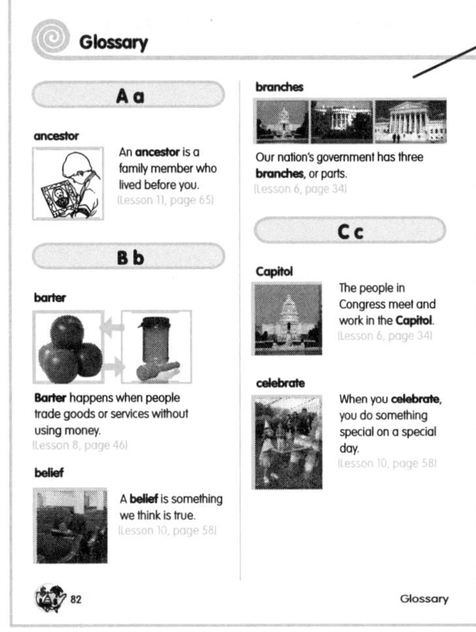

Glossary

A a

ancestor

An **ancestor** is a family member who lived before you.
(Lesson 11, page 65)

B b

barter

Barter happens when people trade goods or services without using money.
(Lesson 8, page 46)

belief

A **belief** is something we think is true.
(Lesson 10, page 58)

branches

Our nation's government has three **branches**, or parts.
(Lesson 6, page 34)

C c

Capitol

The people in Congress meet and work in the **Capitol**.
(Lesson 6, page 34)

celebrate

When you **celebrate**, you do something special on a special day.
(Lesson 10, page 58)

82 Glossary

Glossary

A glossary of the vocabulary words is found at the back of the book. Each entry includes a sentence that defines the word and an illustration, as well as the lesson number and page on which the word first appears.

Teacher Guide

The Teacher Guide for ***Passwords: Social Studies Vocabulary*** contains resources that may be used to introduce, support, and extend students' social studies vocabulary studies. The Teacher Guide includes guided instruction for each student-book lesson.

Multi-Step Lesson Plan

Passwords: Social Studies Vocabulary is built upon the premise that students benefit most from the direct instruction of vocabulary. Each lesson as presented in the Teacher Guide follows a multi-step lesson plan.

1. Introduction of the target vocabulary
2. Activation of students' prior knowledge
3. Provision of the meaning of unknown words
4. Creation by students of visual representations using graphic organizers
5. Further experiences with the target vocabulary
6. Activities that help students retain the word and its meaning

Listening, Speaking, Reading, and Writing

Passwords: Social Studies Vocabulary provides opportunities for students to practice the target vocabulary words while listening, speaking, reading, and writing. These icons indicate opportunities for students to use the vocabulary words in different domains.

 Listening

 Speaking

 Reading

 Writing

Features of the Guided Teaching Lessons

Each lesson of the Teacher Guide contains these features:

- Target Vocabulary with definitions
- Cognates
- Vocabulary Strategy
- Lesson Summary
- Before Reading
- Word and Definition Cards
- Reproduced student book pages
- During Reading
- After Reading
- Annotated student book activity pages
- Extensions
- Ideas for introducing the Write! activity
- Sample answer for Write!
- Word Fun extension

Target Vocabulary

The eight target vocabulary words are listed here with convenient, student-friendly definitions.

LESSON 3 People and the Environment

(Student Book pages 16–21)

Lesson Summary A region is an area that shares some characteristics. Some of these characteristics are weather, climate, and seasons. Water, air, sunlight, and soil are all natural resources found in our environment. Recycling is a way we can preserve our natural resources.

TARGET VOCABULARY

weather what the air is like outside
climate the usual weather of a place over a long time
season a time of year
region an area that shares some features
desert a dry region where there is little rain
natural resources things in nature that people use
environment the natural world around you
recycle to use things again and again

COGNATES

Spanish-speaking students may find a discussion of the similarities and differences between English and Spanish cognates helpful.

English	Spanish
climate	clima
season	estación
region	región
desert	desierto
recycle	reciclar

BEFORE READING

Activate Prior Knowledge

Invite students to look out the window and talk about today's weather. Then ask: Is our weather the same everyday? How can it be different? Is our weather the same in the winter and the summer?

Introduce Target Vocabulary

Tell students they are about to read a selection about weather and some parts of nature. Write the target vocabulary words on the board. Model the pronunciation of each word and have student volunteers repeat the word. Discuss the meaning of each word and, if necessary, write the definition next to the word.

Present Graphic Organizer

Provide each student with a copy of Vocabulary Graphic Organizer: Knowledge Scale, Teacher Guide page 69. Have students write each target vocabulary word in the first column. Then tell them to put a check mark in the column that best identifies their understanding of each word. Have them write the definition of each word as they learn it in the lesson.

Word and Definition Cards for Lesson 3 are on pages 89 and 90 of the Teacher Guide.

VOCABULARY STRATEGY: Context Clues

Review with students the type of context clue in which the author provides the definition of the unknown word, usually using signal words such as "is," "are," or "is called." Have students read the first paragraph of the lesson. Have them locate the words *weather* and *climate*. Point out the context clue "is" following the word *weather* and the words "is called" preceding the word *climate*. Explain how the context clues connect the words to their meanings. As students read, tell them to underline sentences that provide definition context clues and draw an arrow to the word being defined.

26 People and the Environment

Lesson Summary

Use the summary for a quick introduction to the topic of the lesson.

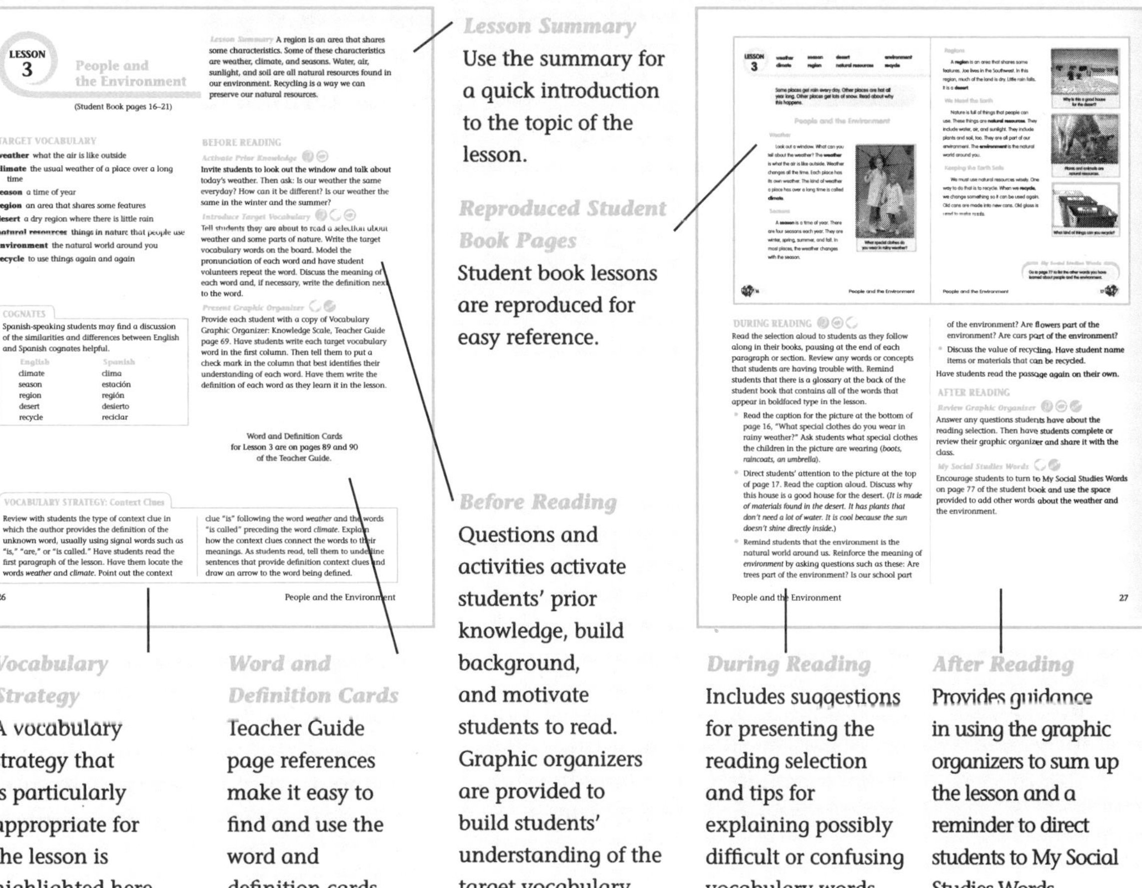

DURING READING

Read the selection aloud to students as they follow along in their books, pausing at the end of each paragraph or section. Review any words or concepts that students are having trouble with. Remind students that there is a glossary at the back of the student book that contains all of the words that appear in boldfaced type in the lesson.

- Read the caption for the picture at the bottom of page 16, "What special clothes do you wear in rainy weather?" Ask students what special clothes the children in the picture are wearing (*boots, raincoats, an umbrella*).
- Direct students' attention to the picture at the top of page 17. Read the caption aloud. Discuss why this house is a good house for the desert. (*It is made of materials found in the desert. It has plants that don't need a lot of water. It is cool because the sun doesn't shine directly inside.*)
- Remind students that the environment is the natural world around us. Reinforce the meaning of *environment* by asking questions such as these: Are trees part of the environment? Is our school part of the environment? Are flowers part of the environment? Are cars part of the environment?
- Discuss the value of recycling. Have student name items or materials that can be recycled.

Have students read the passage again on their own.

AFTER READING

Review Graphic Organizer

Answer any questions students have about the reading selection. Then have students complete or review their graphic organizer and share it with the class.

My Social Studies Words

Encourage students to turn to My Social Studies Words on page 77 of the student book and use the space provided to add other words about the weather and the environment.

People and the Environment 27

Reproduced Student Book Pages

Student book lessons are reproduced for easy reference.

Cognates

Cognates can be a powerful tool in developing the vocabulary of English language learners.

Vocabulary Strategy

A vocabulary strategy that is particularly appropriate for the lesson is highlighted here.

Word and Definition Cards

Teacher Guide page references make it easy to find and use the word and definition cards.

Before Reading

Questions and activities activate students' prior knowledge, build background, and motivate students to read. Graphic organizers are provided to build students' understanding of the target vocabulary.

During Reading

Includes suggestions for presenting the reading selection and tips for explaining possibly difficult or confusing vocabulary words.

After Reading

Provides guidance in using the graphic organizers to sum up the lesson and a reminder to direct students to My Social Studies Words.

Activities

The reproduced student book activity pages are annotated.

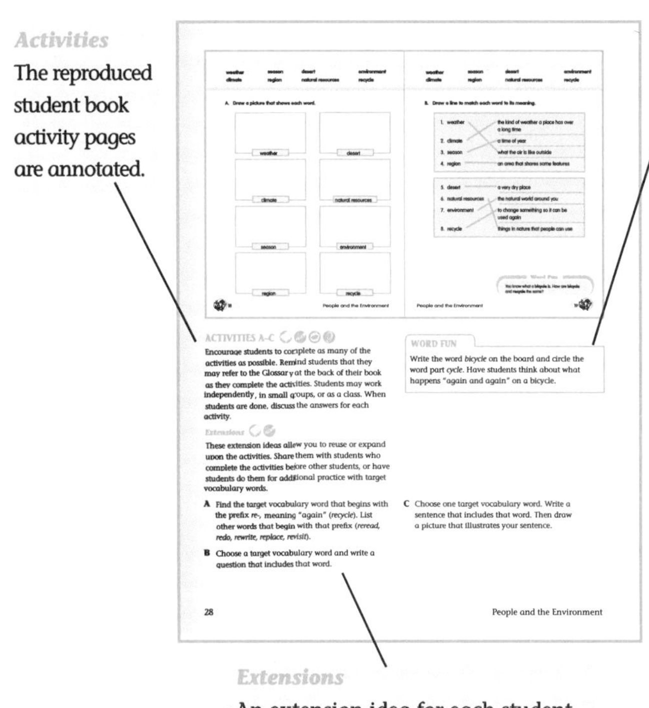

ACTIVITIES A–C

Encourage students to complete as many of the activities as possible. Remind students that they may refer to the Glossary at the back of their book as they complete the activities. Students may work independently, in small groups, or as a class. When students are done, discuss the answers for each activity.

Extensions

These extension ideas allow you to reuse or expand upon the activities. Share them with students who complete the activities before other students, or have students do them for additional practice with target vocabulary words.

A Find the target vocabulary word that begins with the prefix *re-*, meaning "again" (*recycle*). List other words that begin with that prefix (*reread, redo, rewrite, replace, revisit*).

B Choose a target vocabulary word and write a question that includes that word.

C Choose one target vocabulary word. Write a sentence that includes that word. Then draw a picture that illustrates your sentence.

WORD FUN

Write the word *bicycle* on the board and circle the word part *cycle*. Have students think about what happens "again and again" on a bicycle.

28 People and the Environment

Word Fun

Provides additional information about the word highlighted in the student book.

Write!

Each guided lesson provides hints about presenting the **Write!** activity as well as a sample answer.

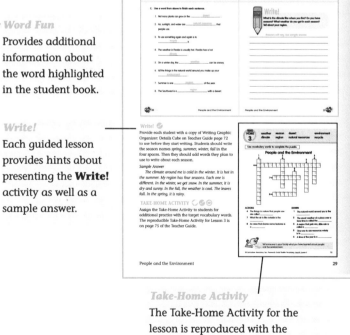

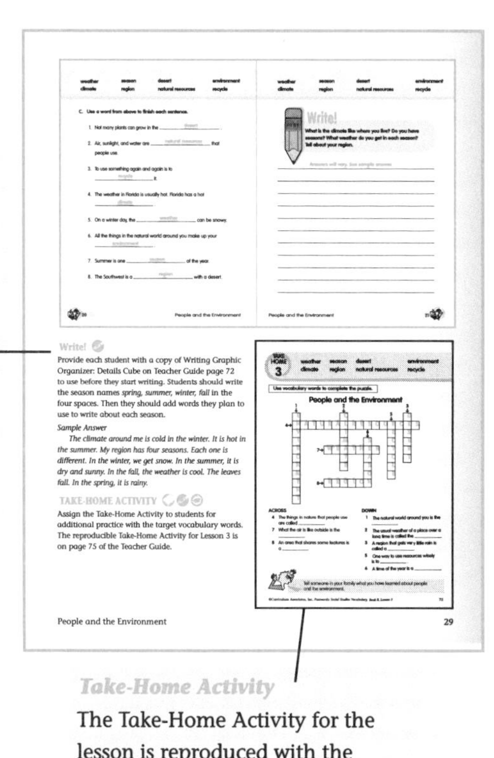

Write!

Provide each student with a copy of Writing Graphic Organizer: Details Cube on Teacher Guide page 72 to use before they start writing. Students should write the season names *spring, summer, winter,* fall in the four spaces. Then they should add words they plan to use to write about each season.

Sample Answer

The climate around me is cold in the winter. It is hot in the summer. My region has four seasons. Each one is different. In the winter, we get snow. In the summer, it is dry and sunny. In the fall, the weather is cool. The leaves fall. In the spring, it is rainy.

TAKE-HOME ACTIVITY

Assign the Take-Home Activity to students for additional practice with the target vocabulary words. The reproducible Take-Home Activity for Lesson 3 is on page 75 of the Teacher Guide.

People and the Environment 29

Extensions

An extension idea for each student book activity allows the activities to be reused or expanded.

Take-Home Activity

The Take-Home Activity for the lesson is reproduced with the answers provided.

Other Teacher Guide Features

- **Vocabulary Teaching Strategies**
  Information and tips about how to employ vocabulary teaching strategies that have proven effective with struggling learners and English language learners begin on page 11.

- **Research Summary**
  A summary of the research that forms the basis of ***Passwords: Social Studies Vocabulary*** is on pages 14–17.

- **Reproducibles**
  Pages 67–108 of the Teacher Guide contain reproducibles for you to share with students.

Graphic Organizers

You may either photocopy the graphic organizers for students to use or use the sample graphic organizer as a model for students to create their own. The Before Reading section of each guided lesson suggests a particular vocabulary graphic organizer to use with the lesson. The Write! section of each guided lesson suggests a writing graphic organizer to use with the Write! activity.

- **Vocabulary Graphic Organizers**

  Four Square This graphic organizer asks students to draw a picture of the word, list examples, write their own definition, and use the word in a sentence.

  Word Web Students write the targeted word or topic in the central circle. They then add information about the word or topic in the outer circles. Students may use the circles to draw a picture, write a definition, list examples, or use the word in a sentence.

  Knowledge Scale This graphic organizer asks students to rate their knowledge of target vocabulary words. It also provides space for students to write a definition of each word after they have mastered its meaning.

- **Writing Graphic Organizers**

  Main Idea and Details Chart This graphic organizer may be used with a variety of writing tasks. Students write a main idea in one box and the details that support it in another box.

  Web A web can be used with a variety of types of writing. Generally, students write the topic, or main idea, of their writing in the upper circle and important points or supporting details in the lower circles.

  Details Cube Students can use each square of the cube to write or draw details that support the main idea of their writing.

Take-Home Activities

Each student book lesson has a take-home activity for additional practice and an opportunity for students to share what they have learned with family members.

Word and Definition Cards

Word cards for each target vocabulary word as well as cards with the definitions for the words are on pages 85–108 of this Teacher Guide. You may either cut the cards out of the book or photocopy them, cut them apart, and then use them. For ideas on how to use the word and definition cards, see page 12 of this Teacher Guide.

Vocabulary Teaching Strategies

These teaching strategies have been shown to be effective with English language learners, but all students who are studying vocabulary will find them helpful.

Accessing Prior Knowledge

Like their English-speaking peers, English language learners come to the classroom with a large body of knowledge. The challenge as a teacher of English language learners is tapping into this knowledge. Before introducing a lesson topic, ask students what they already know about the subject. By doing this, you not only acknowledge students' experiences, but you also find out what information and misinformation students have about the topic. This will enable you to plan a more relevant and focused lesson. Each student book lesson of ***Passwords: Social Studies Vocabulary*** begins with an introductory paragraph written to tap into students' prior knowledge and to provide motivation for reading. In addition, this Teacher Guide includes a prior knowledge activity for each lesson.

Picture File

Use magazines or Web sources to create a file of pictures for each topic. Students will enjoy looking for pictures and pasting them to construction paper. Use the pictures to illustrate target vocabulary words or key concepts. Pictures can be used before, during, or after reading in matching games, gallery walks, and as writing prompts.

Graphic Organizers

This Teacher Guide includes three vocabulary graphic organizers and three writing graphic organizers that can be reproduced for use by students. (See pages 67–72.)

Vocabulary graphic organizers can provide students with a visual representation of a word's meaning by showing examples, synonyms, drawings, descriptions, or the definition of the word. Students can add to the graphic organizer as their understanding of the word increases.

Writing graphic organizers help students organize their thoughts and plan their writing. The writing graphic organizers included in this Teacher Guide are intended for use with different kinds of Write! activities.

Total Physical Response

Total Physical Response, or TPR, is a language-teaching method first developed by Dr. James Asher, a professor of psychology. Asher based his method on his observations of how children learn their native language. In TPR, teachers replace parents, modeling verbal commands, while students respond physically. As a language-teaching method, TPR emphasizes listening and physical response over written language. It has been found to be an effective method for teaching vocabulary. In using TPR to teach vocabulary, teachers and students use movement to associate a word with its meaning. For example, to teach the target vocabulary word *island,* have one student stand in the middle of the room with other students in a circle around him or her. To teach the word *skyscraper,* have students raise their arms and try to touch, or scrape, the sky. To use TPR in your classroom, give commands that require a physical response from students. When they are ready, students can reverse roles, giving commands to you and to fellow students.

Context Clues

Students need to be directly instructed on how to use context clues to help them figure out the meaning of unknown words. There are several different kinds of context clues.

- **Definition**
  In this type of context clue, a definition, or restatement, of the unknown word is provided in the text. Words that signal a definition context clue include *means, is called,* or *is.* Definition context clues are frequently used in ***Passwords: Social Studies Vocabulary***.

- **Synonym**
  Writers sometimes use familiar words with similar meanings to build meaning for an unknown or unfamiliar word.

- **Example**
  Point out to students that writers will sometimes provide an example that will help them figure out the meaning of an unfamiliar word. Words that may signal an example include *like, these, for example,* and *such as.*

Cognates

Cognates are words in different languages that resemble one another in both sound and meaning. Spanish and English have many cognates. Some cognates are spelled identically, although pronunciation differs; for example the words *capital, tractor,* and *radio*. Others are spelled similarly; *valley* and *valle*. Other words that seem similar are not cognates at all. *Bigote* does not mean "bigot"; it means "mustache."

Teachers cannot assume that Spanish-speaking students will automatically or correctly connect an English word with a Spanish cognate. To help students develop the ability to recognize cognates, each ***Passwords: Social Studies Vocabulary*** Teacher Guide lesson includes a list of the Spanish cognates for the target vocabulary in that lesson. As you discuss these cognates with students, point out spelling patterns, such as *-tion* (English) and *-ción* (Spanish). This will help students develop generalizations about language patterns and enhance their ability to use their knowledge of their native language to learn English. Encourage your Spanish-speaking students to guess at the meaning of words in English based on their knowledge of Spanish. If you read the selections aloud, ask Spanish speakers to indicate when they think they hear a cognate. If students read the selections themselves, have them write down the words they think might be cognates. Discuss possible cognates when students have finished reading the selection. Write the word pairs on the board and have students come to the board and circle the similarities between the two words. Have students look for patterns. Students who speak languages other than Spanish may also be able to find English cognates of words from their native languages.

Word Cards

This Teacher Guide includes reproducible word and definition cards on pages 85–108. Each page contains one lesson's words or definitions. These cards can be used in teacher-led and small group activities to introduce new vocabulary and to review vocabulary and concepts. Word cards are helpful to visual, kinesthetic, and aural learners. Word cards provide students with visual cues and constant reinforcement. Many word card activities require you to create copies of the cards. You can photocopy the cards on cardstock or on plain paper. If you want to use the cards as flashcards, with the definition on the back, photocopy the pages as two-sided copies. For many activities, however, you will need cards with one blank side and the word or the definition on the other side. After you make the copies, cut the cards apart. Store the cards in labeled plastic zipper bags for easy access. If you want to provide each student with a set of cards, you might consider having students create their own cards using blank 3½ × 5 file cards. Although you will certainly come up with many ideas of how to use these cards on your own, here are a few activities to begin with.

- **Word Wall**
  A Word Wall can be a great tool in helping students learn vocabulary. Although words are generally displayed on a bulletin board, you can also use more portable display surfaces, such as a shower curtain or a trifold board. Add words to the Word Wall as you introduce the target vocabulary. Review the words daily. Change the words as you begin a new lesson. Word Walls lend themselves to a variety of activities.

  #### Five Clues

  Have each student number their paper from one to five. Give a clue about one of the words on the Word Wall. Students should write down the word they think you are thinking of. Keep giving clues (up to five) until everyone has guessed the word you were thinking of.

Lights On!

You'll need a flashlight for this activity. Turn off the classroom lights. Then point the flashlight at one word on the Word Wall. Call on a student to read the word and either use it in a sentence or provide the definition. When the student is successful, it is his or her turn to point the flashlight at a word and choose another student to read the word.

Wordo

Provide each student with a bingo-type grid with six blank spaces. Tell students to fill in the blanks with words from the Word Wall. Put the corresponding definition cards into a jar. Pull the definition cards from the jar one by one. Read the definition and have students cover the corresponding word on their grid with a marker. When the entire card is covered, Wordo!

- **Card Games**

  The word cards can be used in many different card games, some of which are variations of games played with regular playing cards. Here are a few ideas for games using the word cards.

Concentration

The object of this game is to find matching pairs. Prepare two sets of cards. One set of cards has the vocabulary words and the other set has the definitions. Prepare from 10 cards (for 5 matches) to 30 cards (15 matches). Mix up the two sets of cards. Place the cards face down in rows. Players take turns turning over pairs of cards. If the cards match, the player makes a sentence using the vocabulary word. If the cards don't match, play goes to the next player. If the student successfully creates a sentence using the vocabulary word, he or she goes again. The player with the most cards at the end is the winner.

Guess the Word

This game is for four students, playing in pairs. Prepare a card for each vocabulary word. Put the cards face down in the middle of the table. The first student of the first pair picks a card and gives a one-word clue to his or her partner that will enable the partner to guess the target vocabulary word. If the partner does not guess the word, the word goes to a member of the other pair who gives a hint to his or her partner. The team that successfully guesses the word keeps the card. The team with the most cards wins.

What Is the Need for *Passwords: Social Studies Vocabulary*?

Learning academic vocabulary is essential to each student's comprehension of content-area materials. Researchers (Bailey, 2007; Resnick, 2006; Ogle, Klemp, & McBride, 2007; Yarbrough, 2007) have shown that many content-area texts may present learning barriers to students. In a 2006 textbook survey by Education Market Research, teachers were asked about the biggest problems they experienced with their current text. Teachers stated that texts that are "hard for students to read" (35.2%) was the biggest problem, followed closely by "doesn't meet needs of diverse students" (31.4%). Several factors may make a text hard to read, such as:

- A textbook analysis found that some texts are written approximately 2 to 4 reading levels above grade level. This fact highlights why students may struggle with content-area instructional materials (Yarbrough, 2007).
- Social studies texts are more lexically dense and the wording of these texts are not typical to what students hear and say in everyday life (Bailey, 2007).
- Background knowledge of a topic may not be incorporated into a new lesson, causing a disconnect for students who are not familiar with a specific social-studies topic (Ogle, Klemp, & McBride, 2007).
- Struggling readers have difficulty with nonlinear reading. Excess use of photographs, charts, maps, and graphs can inhibit rather than support a struggling reader's comprehension (Ogle, Klemp, & McBride, 2007).

Concerns about students' comprehension of content-area texts continues to grow. The 2006 National Assessment of Educational Progress (NAEP) Social Studies Assessment reported minor increases in the "Basic" level of performance of 4th- and 8th-grade students (Lee & Weiss, 2007). While these results are encouraging, the reauthorization of the No Child Left Behind Act (NCLB) proposes to make NAEP results even more significant. Under the NCLB reauthorization, NAEP assessment scores will be listed alongside each state's scores. This comparison of scores is meant to close the achievement gap between state tests and the NAEP tests (U.S. Department of Ed., 2007). This new initiative heightens the need for students to master academic vocabulary for better comprehension of content-area materials.

Passwords: Social Studies Vocabulary is a tool that can support students who struggle with "hard-to-read" texts. It unites students with a singular goal of successfully learning the academic language of social studies. This goal is attainable through the instructional features and strategies that research has proven to be effective with diverse student populations.

Why Is *Passwords: Social Studies Vocabulary* Helpful to ELL Students?

Academic language proficiency is the ability of the student to comprehend, speak, read, and write when the context is reduced and the topic is cognitively demanding. Examples of cognitively demanding activities are reading textbooks, writing long compositions, learning new concepts, and mastering local and state requirements that test students on the academic language of each content area. Zelasko & Antunez (2000) state that "without mastery of classroom English, they [ELL students] will have difficulty competing academically in an all-English setting." The importance of learning academic language is confirmed by additional researchers (August, Carlo, Dressler, & Snow, 2005):

- "Vocabulary development is one of the greatest challenges to reading instruction for ELLs, because in order to read fluently and comprehend what is written, students need to use not just phonics, but context" (Antunez, 2002).
- "For English language learners, academic English is like a third language, their second language being the social English of the hallways, community, and media. And whereas students are exposed to social English in various settings, academic language acquisition is generally limited to the classroom. . . . Many English language learners, even those with well-developed social language, struggle to master the complex language of school" (Zwiers, 2004/2005).

What Are the Strategies and Features in *Passwords: Social Studies Vocabulary* that Research Has Proven to Be Effective with ELL Students?

Social studies is a cognitively demanding school subject. In addition, the vocabulary of social studies is also considered as Tier III vocabulary, which requires direct and explicit instruction (Beck, McKeown, & Kucan, 2002). This is especially important for ELL students. The first step to comprehending the content of a school subject is to understand the vocabulary and language of the school subject. ***Passwords: Social Studies Vocabulary*** incorporates ELL instructional recommendations from content-area experts for teaching vocabulary.

Marzano & Pickering (2005), in *Building Academic Vocabulary*, promote a six-step process for teaching new terms. This process is also integrated in ***Passwords: Social Studies Vocabulary***.

Step 1: Provide a description, an explanation, or an example of the new term (along with a nonlinguistic representation).

Step 2: Ask students to restate the description, explanation, or example in their own words.

Step 3: Ask students to construct a picture, symbol, or graphic representing the term.

Step 4: Engage students periodically in activities that help them add to their knowledge of the terms.

Step 5: Engage students periodically to discuss the terms with one another.

Step 6: Involve students periodically in games that allow them to play with terms.

Additionally, educational experts and researchers from numerous professional organizations (Association for Supervision and Curriculum Developers, English Language Summit, and International Reading Association) have created a list of instructional recommendations that have been found to be effective, especially with ELL students. While these organizations are separate entities, they share some common recommendations. These recommendations are integrated throughout ***Passwords: Social Studies Vocabulary***.

***Passwords: Social Studies Vocabulary* Uses . . .**	**Research Says . . .**
Direct Instruction Within Context (SB, Reading Passage & Activities A–D)	*"The teaching of individual words is most effective when learners are given both definitional and contextual information, when learners actively process the new word meanings, and when they experience multiple encounters with words" (Graves & Watts-Taffe, 2002).*
Prior-Knowledge Activation (SB, Prereading Activity; TG)	*"To facilitate communication of content knowledge, teachers can offer support in several ways: Plan adequate time to activate students' prior knowledge and encourage students to share what they already know in journals, small groups, or paired brainstorming sessions" (Rolón, 2002/2003).*
Collaborative Learning (SB, Prereading Activity & Activities A–D; TG)	*"Students interacting verbally with other native speakers of English pick up vocabulary and content knowledge" (Association of American Publishers, 2004).* *"Research and common sense . . . confirm that interacting with other people about what we are learning deepens the understanding of everyone involved—particularly when we are learning new terms" (Marzano & Pickering, 2005).*
Differentiated Instruction (SB, Activities A–D; TG)	*"Numerous theorists and contemporary translators of brain research propose that students do not learn effectively when tasks are too simple or too complex for their particular readiness levels. Rather, say these researchers, tasks must be moderately challenging for the individual for growth to occur" (Tomlinson, 2004).*
Parental Engagement (TG, Take-Home Activities)	*"The evidence is consistent, positive, and convincing: families have a major influence on their children's achievement in school and through life" (Henderson & Mapp, 2002).*
Total Physical Response (TG, Vocabulary Teaching Strategies section, During Reading Activity)	*"Having children physically act out songs, poems, or readings—all forms of TPR methodology—is an effective way to support vocabulary development" (Drucker, 2003).* *In a research synthesis, Slavin & Cheung (2005) state that teachers of English language learners may use language development strategies, such as total physical response, to help students internalize new vocabulary.*

(Continues)

(Continued)

***Passwords: Social Studies Vocabulary* Uses . . .**	**Research Says . . .**
Considerate Text (SB, Reading Passages)	*"Certain features of text make it more 'considerate,' or easier to read and understand. The features should have clear concepts, consistent text structure, references that are easy to locate, and vocabulary that is precise and relates clearly to the subject. . . . A considerate text makes comprehension easier" (Dyck & Pemberton, 2002).*
Graphic Organizers (Semantic Feature Analysis & Semantic Mapping) (TG, Pre- & Post-reading Activities)	*Hedrick, Harmon, & Linerode (2004, 2000) have analyzed content-area textbooks and have concluded that "textbooks infrequently include visual representations of concepts as a vocabulary instructional strategy."*
Clear and Explicit Illustrations and Artwork (SB, Reading Passages)	*"Giving an ESL student a nonlinguistic representation will provide a way for them to understand the meaning of the term that is not dependent on an understanding of English" (Marzano & Pickering, 2005).*
Deep Word-Study Activities (Roots, Prefixes, Suffixes, Cognates) (SB/TG)	*Students may find learning English easier if there are similar roots and pre/suffixes between their first language and English. Hansen (2006) suggests exploring cognates in order to aid students in making connections between their first language and English.* *"Teaching a word's facets of meaning moves students beyond a narrow definition of a word" (Beck, McKeown, & Kucan, 2002).*
Word Play Activities (TG, Take-Home Activities, Word Cards)	*Researchers (Marzano & Pickering, 2005; Paynter, Bodrova, & Doty, 2005; Richek, 2005) stress that word play builds a strong connection to newly learned vocabulary.* *"Activities using words in games, connecting words, and manipulating words creatively result in excellent student learning" (Beck, McKeown, & Kucan, 2002).*
Association/ Connection Methods: (Personal Connection, Picture Connection, Word Connection) (SB/TG, throughout each lesson, Glossary)	*"This step is particularly important to ESL students. Whereas they might be constrained in their ability to devise a linguistic description, explanation, or example, they will not be constrained in their ability to create a nonlinguistic representation . . . These representations will most likely reflect the students' native culture, which is exactly the intent. Learning academic terms involves making connections with things familiar to us, and these things commonly arise from experiences native to our culture" (Marzano & Pickering, 2005).*
Modeling Through Audio (*Passwords* Audio CD)	*"When English language learners can simultaneously hear and read content-related information . . . it helps them decipher the text structures commonly found in textbooks" (Rubinstein-Ávila, 2006).*
Read Alouds (TG)	*"Teacher read-alouds are perhaps the most consistent activity used by classroom teachers that provides frequent, if not daily, opportunities to enhance the literacy of ELLs by integrating effective vocabulary development practices" (Hickman, Pollard-Durodola, & Vaughn, 2004).*
Speaking, Listening, Reading, Writing Experiences (SB/TG, throughout each lesson)	*"Successful word learning is active. Students learn words by using them. Thinking, saying, and writing new words help us make new words our own" (Bromley, 2003).* *García (1999) recommended that teachers use ". . . curriculum materials that are rich in opportunities for speaking, listening, reading, and writing in English."*

References

Antunez, B. (2002). English language learners and the five essential components of reading comprehension. Accessed February 27, 2006, from http://www.readingrockets.org/articles/341#vocab.

Association of American Publishers. (Fall 2004). English Language Learners summit proceedings, AAP School Division. Summit on English Language Learners. The Washington Court Hotel, Washington, DC. October 12, 2004. Accessed January 16, 2006, from http://www.publishers.org/SchoolDiv/research/research_03/research_03_Rep_05.htm.

August, D., Carlo, M., Dressler, C., & Snow, C. (2005). The critical role of vocabulary development for English language learners. *Learning Disabilities Research & Practice, 20*(1), 50–57.

Bailey, A. L. (Ed.). (2007). *The language demands of school: Putting academic English to the test.* New Haven: Yale University Press.

Beck, I. L., McKeown, M. G., & Kucan, L. (2002). *Bringing words to life: Robust vocabulary instruction.* New York: Guilford Press.

Bromley, K. (2003, April). Vocabulary S-t-r-e-t-c-h-e-r-s, *Instructor, 112*(7).

Drucker, M. J. (2003). What reading teachers should know about ESL learners: Good teaching is teaching for all. *The Reading Teacher, 57*(1).

Dyck, N., & Pemberton, J. B. (2002). A model for making decisions about text adaptations. *Intervention in School & Clinic, 38*(1).

García, E. (1999). *Student cultural diversity: Understanding and meeting the challenge* (2nd ed.). Boston: Houghton Mifflin.

Graves, M. F., & Watts-Taffe, S. M. (2002). The place of word consciousness in a research-based vocabulary program in *What research has to say about reading instruction.* Newark, DE: International Reading Association.

Hedrick, W. B., Harmon, J. M., & Linerode, P. M. (2004). Teachers' beliefs and practices of vocabulary instruction with social studies textbooks in Grades 4–8. *Reading Horizons, 45*(2), 103–125.

Hedrick, W. B., Harmon, J. M., & Linerode, P. M. (2000). Content analysis of vocabulary instruction in social studies textbooks for grades 4–8. *Elementary School Journal, 100*(3), 253–271.

Henderson, A. T., & Mapp, K. L. (2002). *A new wave of evidence: The impact of school, family, and community connections on student achievement. Annual Synthesis 2002.* National Center for Family & Community Connections with Schools. Austin: Southwest Educational Development Laboratory.

Hickman, P., Pollard-Durodola, S., & Vaughn, S. (2004). Storybook reading: Improving vocabulary and comprehension for English-language learners. *Reading Teacher, 57*(8), 720–730.

Lee, J., & Weiss, A. (2007). *The Nation's Report Card: U.S. History 2006* (NCES 2007–474). U.S. Department of Education, National Center for Education Statistics. Washington, DC: U.S. Government Printing Office.

Marzano, R. J., & Pickering, D. J. (2005). *Building Academic Vocabulary: Teacher's manual.* Alexandria, VA: ASCD.

Ogle, D., Klemp, R., & McBride, B. (2007). *Building literacy in social studies: Strategies for improving comprehension and critical thinking.* Washington, DC: Association for Supervision and Curriculum Development.

Paynter, D. E., Bodrova, E., & Doty, J. K. (2005). *For the love of words: Vocabulary instruction that works, grades K–6.* San Francisco: Jossey-Bass.

Resnick, B. (2006). Social studies market, Grades K–12. Rockaway Park, NY: Education Market Research.

Richek, M. A. (2005, February). Words are wonderful: Interactive, time-efficient strategies to teach meaning vocabulary. *Reading Teacher, 58*(5), 414–423.

Rolón, C. A. (2002/2003). Educating Latino students. *Educational Leadership, 60*(4), 40–3.

Rubinstein-Ávila, E. (2006). Connecting with Latino Learners. *Educational Leadership, 63*(5), 38–43.

Slavin, R. E., & Cheung, A. (2005). Synthesis of research on language of reading instruction for English language learners. *Review of Educational Research Summer, 75*(2), 247–284.

Tomlinson, C. A. (2004, April). Differentiation in diverse settings. *School Administrator, 61*(7).

U.S. Department of Education. (2004). *Parental involvement: Title One, Part A Non-regulatory guidance.* Washington, DC: No Child Left Behind.

U.S. Department of Education, *Building on Results: A Blueprint for Strengthening the No Child Left Behind Act,* Washington, DC, 2007.

Yarbrough, B. (2007). Why Johnny Can't Read His Textbook. *Hesperia Star.* Accessed April 25, 2007, from http://www.hesperiastar.com/onset?id=656&template=article.html.

Zelasko, N., & Antunez, B. (2000). *If your child learns in two languages: A parent's guide for improving educational opportunities for children acquiring English as a second language.* National Clearinghouse of Bilingual Education: The George Washington University: Graduate School of Education and Human Development. Washington, DC.

Zwiers, J. (2004/2005). The third language of academic English. *Educational Leadership, 62*(4), 60–63.

Land and Water

(Student Book pages 4–9)

Lesson Summary Geography is the study of Earth's land and water. Land has many shapes, known as landforms. Mountains, valleys, and islands are three different landforms. Most of Earth's water is in its oceans. Lakes and rivers are other bodies of water.

TARGET VOCABULARY

geography the study of Earth's land and water
landform any kind of land with any shape
mountain the highest kind of land
valley low land between mountains
island land with water all around it
ocean a very large body of salt water
lake water with land all around it
river water that flows across land

COGNATES

Spanish-speaking students may find a discussion of the similarities and differences between English and Spanish cognates helpful.

English	Spanish
geography	geografía
mountain	montaña
valley	valle
island	isla
ocean	océano
lake	lago

BEFORE READING

Activate Prior Knowledge 

Flip through the pages of a textbook or a magazine, looking for photographs that show scenes that include mountains, valleys, oceans, lakes, and rivers. As you find these things, ask students to name them and decide whether they are pictures of land or water. Then discuss the characteristics of each landform or body of water.

Introduce Target Vocabulary 

Tell students they are about to read a selection about Earth's land and water. Write the target vocabulary words on the board. Model the pronunciation of each word and have student volunteers repeat the word. Discuss the meaning of each word and, if necessary, write the definition next to the word.

Present Graphic Organizer 

Provide each student with a copy of Vocabulary Graphic Organizer: Four Square, Teacher Guide page 67. Have students choose or assign each student a target vocabulary word. Tell students to write their word in the center square. As they read, students should add information about the target word to the graphic organizer.

Word and Definition Cards for Lesson 1 are on pages 85 and 86 of the Teacher Guide.

VOCABULARY STRATEGY: Context Clues

Tell students that writers sometimes provide a definition, or the meaning of a word, right before or right after the word is introduced. For example, in the sentence "Boulders are very large rocks," the author directly provides the definition of *boulders*.

Tell students that words such as *is*, *are*, *means*, and *is called* near the new word may signal a definition context clue. Ask students to circle the definition context clues they find in this lesson and draw an arrow to the word that each clue defines.

LESSON 1

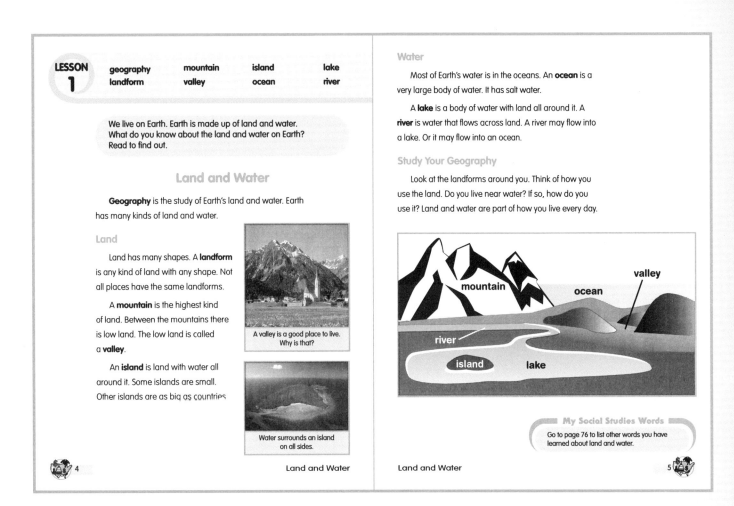

geography	mountain	island	lake
landform	valley	ocean	river

We live on Earth. Earth is made up of land and water. What do you know about the land and water on Earth? Read to find out.

Land and Water

Geography is the study of Earth's land and water. Earth has many kinds of land and water.

Land

Land has many shapes. A **landform** is any kind of land with any shape. Not all places have the same landforms.

A **mountain** is the highest kind of land. Between the mountains there is low land. The low land is called a **valley**.

A valley is a good place to live. Why is that?

An **island** is land with water all around it. Some islands are small. Other islands are as big as countries.

Water surrounds an island on all sides.

Water

Most of Earth's water is in the oceans. An **ocean** is a very large body of water. It has salt water.

A **lake** is a body of water with land all around it. A **river** is water that flows across land. A river may flow into a lake. Or it may flow into an ocean.

Study Your Geography

Look at the landforms around you. Think of how you use the land. Do you live near water? If so, how do you use it? Land and water are part of how you live every day.

mountain
valley
ocean
river
island
lake

My Social Studies Words

Go to page 76 to list other words you have learned about land and water.

DURING READING

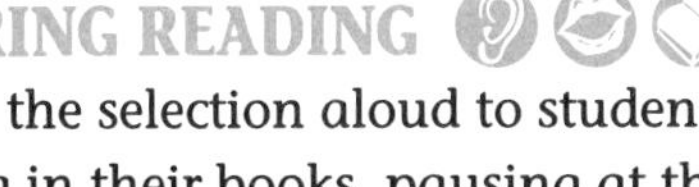

Read the selection aloud to students as they follow along in their books, pausing at the end of each paragraph or section. Review any words or concepts that students are having trouble with. Remind students that there is a glossary at the back of the student book that contains all of the words that appear in boldfaced type in the lesson.

- Write the word *geography* on the board. Circle each syllable. Guide students to pronounce the word as they tap out the syllables with their fingers. Then have students say the word and use it in a sentence.
- Write the word *valley* on the board in large letters. Tell students that the *v* at the beginning of *valley* can help them remember what a valley is. Trace the *v* several times, pointing out that the letter *v* is in the shape of a valley. The sides of the letter are like two tall mountains and the bottom of the letter is the low land, or the valley, between the mountains.
- Write the word *island* on the board and circle the letter *s*. Explain that the *s* in *island* is silent.
- Ask students to tell how an ocean is different from a lake. Then ask them to tell how a lake is different from a river.

Have students read the passage again on their own.

AFTER READING

Review Graphic Organizer

Answer any questions students have about the reading selection. Then have students complete or review their graphic organizer and share it with the class.

My Social Studies Words

Encourage students to turn to My Social Studies Words on page 76 of the student book and use the space provided to add other words about land and water.

geography mountain island lake
landform valley ocean river

A. Circle the word that goes with each picture.

1. river / valley / (island)
2. (mountain) / ocean / lake
3. river / (landform) / lake
4. mountain / (lake) / geography
5. valley / landform / (ocean)
6. (river) / valley / island
7. (geography) / ocean / lake
8. island / ocean / (valley)

6 Land and Water

geography mountain island lake
landform valley ocean river

B. Draw a line to match each word to its meaning.

1. geography — any kind of land with any shape
2. landform — the highest kind of land
3. mountain — low land between mountains
4. valley — the study of Earth's land and water

5. island — a very large body of salt water
6. ocean — water that flows across land
7. lake — land with water all around it
8. river — a body of water with land all around it

Word Fun

The word **landform** is made of two small words. What are they?

Land and Water 7

ACTIVITIES A–C

Encourage students to complete as many of the activities as possible. Remind students that they may refer to the Glossary at the back of their book as they complete the activities. Students may work independently, in small groups, or as a class. When students are done, discuss the answers for each activity.

Extensions 

These extension ideas allow you to reuse or expand upon the activities. Share them with students who complete the activities before other students, or have students do them for additional practice with target vocabulary words.

A Write the vocabulary words in alphabetical order.

B Choose one of these target vocabulary words: *geography, landform, mountain*. Make as many smaller words as you can, using only the letters found in the word you chose.

C Choose one target vocabulary word. Write a sentence that includes that word. Then draw a picture that illustrates your sentence.

WORD FUN

Remind students that the word *landform* is made from the two small words *land* and *form*. Write the compound word *landslide* on the board. Ask students to circle the two small words in it. Then guide them to use the meanings of the small words to figure out what a landslide is.

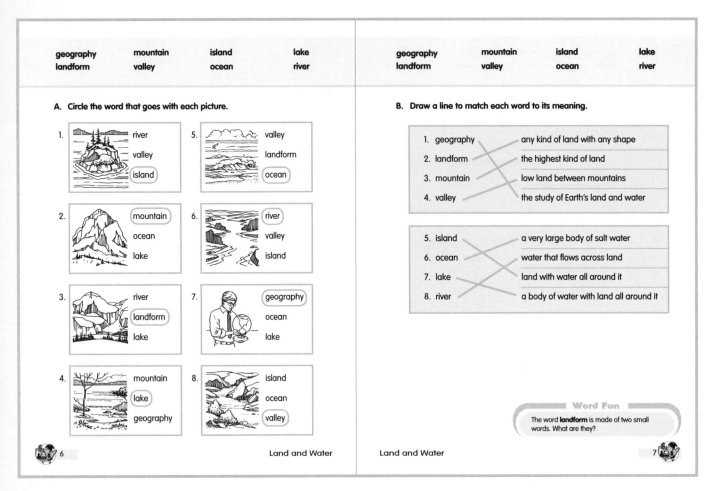

geography landform mountain valley island ocean lake river

C. Use a word from above to finish each sentence.

1. The highest land on Earth is a mountain.
2. A big ship sailed toward an island in the ocean.
3. There is land all around a lake.
4. The study of land and water is called geography.
5. Big waves and salt water are part of an ocean.
6. The low land between mountains is called a valley.
7. A mountain is one type of landform.
8. Water that flows over land is a river.

8 Land and Water

geography landform mountain valley island ocean lake river

Write!

What are the landforms around you? What kind of water is near you? Tell how you use the land and the water.

Answers will vary. See sample answer.

Land and Water 9

Write!

Provide each student with a copy of Writing Graphic Organizer: Main Idea and Details Chart on Teacher Guide page 70 to use before they start writing. Tell students to write "Landforms" in the first Main Idea box. In the Details box, they should write words that tell about the landforms around them and how they use them. In the next Main Idea box, they should write "Water." In the Details box, they should write about the bodies of water around them and how they use them. When students are ready to begin writing, provide a sentence starter such as the following:

I live near a _________.

Sample Answer

I live near a lake. It is not big. But I can go in a boat on the lake. I like to fish in the lake. There are hills and valleys near me too. A lot of the land has rocks. I like to hike over the hills.

TAKE-HOME ACTIVITY 

Assign the Take-Home Activity to students for additional practice with the target vocabulary words. The reproducible Take-Home Activity for Lesson 1 is on page 73 of the Teacher Guide.

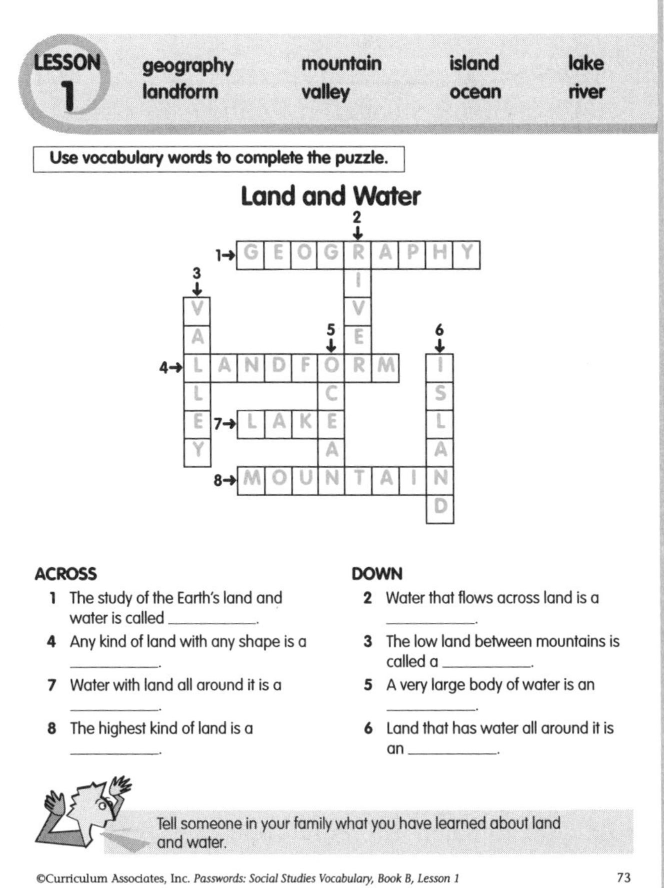

LESSON 1 geography landform mountain valley island ocean lake river

Use vocabulary words to complete the puzzle.

Land and Water

ACROSS

1 The study of the Earth's land and water is called _________.

4 Any kind of land with any shape is a _________.

7 Water with land all around it is a _________.

8 The highest kind of land is a _________.

DOWN

2 Water that flows across land is a _________.

3 The low land between mountains is called a _________.

5 A very large body of water is an _________.

6 Land that has water all around it is an _________.

Tell someone in your family what you have learned about land and water.

 73

LESSON 2 Communities Are Different

(Student Book pages 10–15)

Lesson Summary People live in neighborhoods in communities. Communities can be found in suburbs, urban areas, and rural areas. Each of these places has its own characteristics. Land is divided into meaningful sections. Continents are divided into countries. Our country is divided into states.

TARGET VOCABULARY

community a place where people live

urban area another name for a city

neighborhood part of a city or town

suburb a town near a city

rural area a place with fewer stores or houses than a city or town

continent a large body of land

country a land with the same laws

state a part of a country

COGNATES

Spanish-speaking students may find a discussion of the similarities and differences between English and Spanish cognates helpful.

English	Spanish
community	comunidad
urban	urbano
rural	rural
continent	continente
state	estado

BEFORE READING

Activate Prior Knowledge 

Display a map of the United States and identify it as a country. Use your finger to outline individual states. Ask students what these smaller pieces of the country are called. If you happen to have a puzzle of the United States, with pieces that represent individual states, use it to emphasize that states combine to form a country.

Introduce Target Vocabulary  

Tell students they are about to read a selection about places where people live. Write the target vocabulary words on the board. Model the pronunciation of each word and have student volunteers repeat the word. Discuss the meaning of each word and, if necessary, write the definition next to the word.

Present Graphic Organizer 

Provide each student with a copy of Vocabulary Graphic Organizer: Word Web, Teacher Guide page 68. Assign each student a target vocabulary word. Have students write the word in the center circle of the web. Tell them to draw a picture of the word, write the word's definition, and write a sentence using the word in three of the surrounding circles. In the remaining circle, ask students to write a word they associate with the target vocabulary word.

Word and Definition Cards for Lesson 2 are on pages 87 and 88 of the Teacher Guide.

VOCABULARY STRATEGY: Print Features

Discuss with students why a word might appear in boldfaced, or darker, type in a textbook. (*It is a new word. It is an important word to know.*) Tell students that they can often find the meaning of a boldfaced word close to where the word appears in the text. Direct students' attention to the first paragraph of the lesson. Ask what words are darker than the others (*community, urban area*). Help students locate the meaning of *community* and *urban area* in the paragraph. As they read the lesson, have students draw an arrow from each boldfaced word to the words that explain its meaning.

LESSON 2

community	neighborhood	rural area	country
urban area	suburb	continent	state

Some people live in towns. Other people live in cities. How are these places different? Read to find out.

Communities Are Different

A **community** is a place where people live. Cities and towns are communities. Rico lives in a city. Many people live near him. A city is an **urban area**.

Rico's neighborhood is in an urban area.

Neighborhoods Are Special

A **neighborhood** is a part of a city or town. Not all neighborhoods are the same. Rico's neighborhood has busy streets. It has lots of stores and homes. It has a school and a park.

A **suburb** is a town near a city. It has fewer people than a city has. People in suburbs may work in the city.

Houses in a suburb may be far apart.

10 Communities Are Different

Other Communities

Ann lives in a **rural area**. It has fewer stores or homes than a city or town has. It has fewer people, too.

A rural area has farms.

Lands Are Divided

A **continent** is a large body of land. There are seven continents. Most of them are home to many countries.

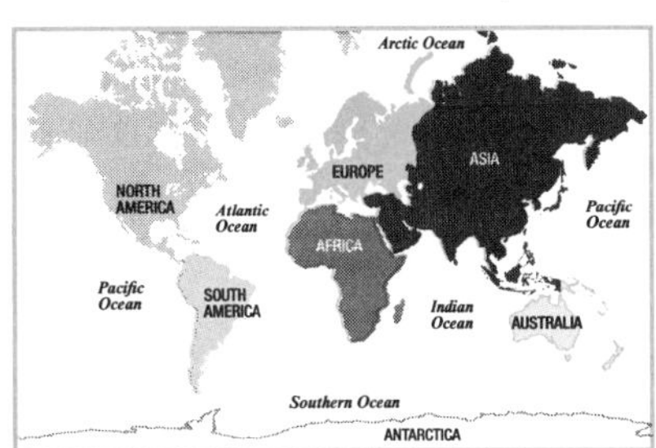

Our country is the United States. A **country** is a land with the same laws. Our country has 50 states. Each **state**, or part, has some urban areas. Most states have suburbs and rural areas, too.

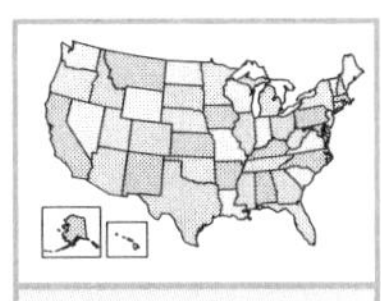

The United States is a country with many states.

My Social Studies Words

Go to page 76 to list other words you have learned about different communities.

Communities Are Different 11

DURING READING 

Read the selection aloud to students as they follow along in their books, pausing at the end of each paragraph or section. Review any words or concepts that students are having trouble with. Remind students that there is a glossary at the back of the student book that contains all of the words that appear in boldfaced type in the lesson.

- Have students study the pictures of the urban area and the suburb on page 10 and the picture of the rural setting on page 11. First, ask students to tell how the urban area is different than the suburb. Then discuss how the suburb is different than the rural area.
- Before students read the text under the heading "Lands Are Divided," discuss the meaning of divided. Tell students that it means "separated into smaller pieces." Help students identify things that can be divided.
- Point out the word body in the second paragraph on page 11. Explain that body is a word that has more than one meaning. Ask students to point to a part of their own body. Then explain that body can also mean "an area of water or land."
- Direct student's attention to the drawing of the continents on page 11. Make sure that students understand that these are continents, not countries.

Have students read the passage again on their own.

AFTER READING

Review Graphic Organizer 

Answer any questions students have about the reading selection. Then have students complete or review their graphic organizer and share it with the class.

My Social Studies Words 

Encourage students to turn to My Social Studies Words on page 76 of the student book and use the space provided to add other words about different communities.

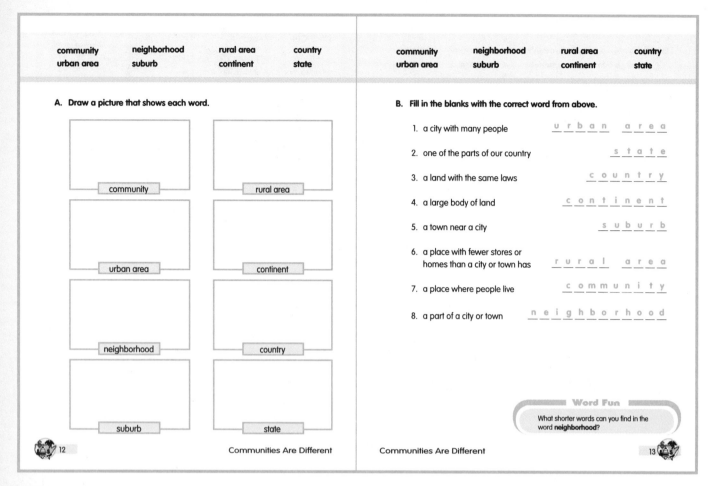

community
urban area
neighborhood
suburb
rural area
continent
country
state

A. Draw a picture that shows each word.

community	rural area
urban area	continent
neighborhood	country
suburb	state

community
urban area
neighborhood
suburb
rural area
continent
country
state

B. Fill in the blanks with the correct word from above.

1. a city with many people u r b a n a r e a
2. one of the parts of our country s t a t e
3. a land with the same laws c o u n t r y
4. a large body of land c o n t i n e n t
5. a town near a city s u b u r b
6. a place with fewer stores or homes than a city or town has r u r a l a r e a
7. a place where people live c o m m u n i t y
8. a part of a city or town n e i g h b o r h o o d

Word Fun

What shorter words can you find in the word **neighborhood**?

ACTIVITIES A–C

Encourage students to complete as many of the activities as possible. Remind students that they may refer to the Glossary at the back of their book as they complete the activities. Students may work independently, in small groups, or as a class. When students are done, discuss the answers for each activity.

Extensions 

These extension ideas allow you to reuse or expand upon the activities. Share them with students who complete the activities before other students, or have students do them for additional practice with target vocabulary words.

A Write as many words as you can that rhyme with the target vocabulary word *state*.

B Divide each target vocabulary word into syllables by drawing lines between the syllables of each word.

C Draw a picture of something in your own neighborhood. Write a caption to go with your picture.

WORD FUN

Have students write the letters in the word *neighborhood* in a vertical column. Then have them try to think of things that can be found in their neighborhood that begin with each letter in the word. Have them write the word next to the letter. Provide time for students to compare their words with one another when they are done.

community urban area neighborhood suburb rural area continent country state

C. **Use a word from above to finish each sentence.**

1. An area with farms is a rural area.
2. There may be many countries on one continent.
3. A community close to a city is a suburb.
4. We live in a country called the United States.
5. One of the parts that make up our country is a state.
6. There are lots of buildings and people in an urban area.
7. A city or a small town is a community.
8. Rico lives in a neighborhood in the city.

14 Communities Are Different

community urban area neighborhood suburb rural area continent country state

Write!

Tell about your community. Is it a rural or urban area? Is it a suburb? Tell what your neighborhood is like.

Answers will vary. See sample answer.

Communities Are Different 15

Write!

Provide each student with a copy of Writing Graphic Organizer: Web on Teacher Guide page 71, to use before they start writing. Students should write "My Neighborhood" in the center circle. In the surrounding circles, they should write words and phrases that describe their neighborhood, including the words *rural, urban area,* or *suburb.* You might want to provide a sentence starter such as the following: *I live in a ________.*

Sample Answer

I live in a suburb. My neighborhood has lots of houses. They are close together. Some people in my neighborhood work in a city that is nearby. There is a park in my neighborhood.

TAKE-HOME ACTIVITY

Assign the Take-Home Activity to students for additional practice with the target vocabulary words. The reproducible Take-Home Activity for Lesson 2 is on page 74 of the Teacher Guide.

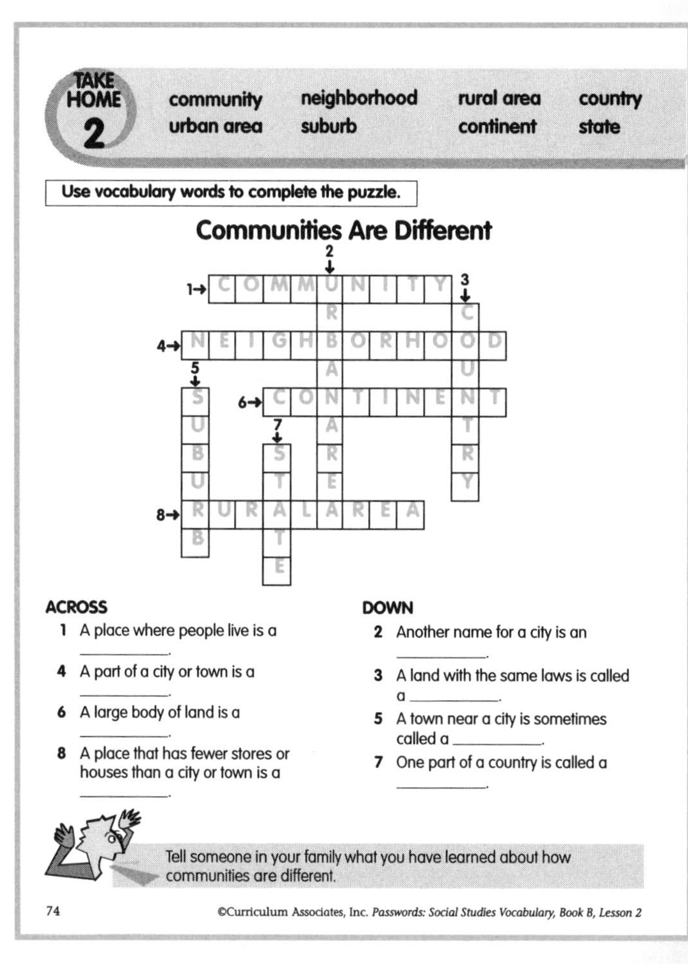

TAKE HOME 2

community urban area neighborhood suburb rural area continent country state

Use vocabulary words to complete the puzzle.

Communities Are Different

ACROSS

1 A place where people live is a ________.

4 A part of a city or town is a ________.

6 A large body of land is a ________.

8 A place that has fewer stores or houses than a city or town is a ________.

DOWN

2 Another name for a city is an ________.

3 A land with the same laws is called a ________.

5 A town near a city is sometimes called a ________.

7 One part of a country is called a ________.

Tell someone in your family what you have learned about how communities are different.

74

LESSON 3

People and the Environment

(Student Book pages 16–21)

Lesson Summary A region is an area that shares some characteristics. Some of these characteristics are weather, climate, and seasons. Water, air, sunlight, and soil are all natural resources found in our environment. Recycling is a way we can preserve our natural resources.

TARGET VOCABULARY

weather what the air is like outside

climate the usual weather of a place over a long time

season a time of year

region an area that shares some features

desert a dry region where there is little rain

natural resources things in nature that people use

environment the natural world around you

recycle to use things again and again

COGNATES

Spanish-speaking students may find a discussion of the similarities and differences between English and Spanish cognates helpful.

English	Spanish
climate	clima
season	estación
region	región
desert	desierto
recycle	reciclar

BEFORE READING

Activate Prior Knowledge

Invite students to look out the window and talk about today's weather. Then ask: Is our weather the same everyday? How can it be different? Is our weather the same in the winter and the summer?

Introduce Target Vocabulary

Tell students they are about to read a selection about weather and some parts of nature. Write the target vocabulary words on the board. Model the pronunciation of each word and have student volunteers repeat the word. Discuss the meaning of each word and, if necessary, write the definition next to the word.

Present Graphic Organizer

Provide each student with a copy of Vocabulary Graphic Organizer: Knowledge Scale, Teacher Guide page 69. Have students write each target vocabulary word in the first column. Then tell them to put a check mark in the column that best identifies their understanding of each word. Have them write the definition of each word as they learn it in the lesson.

Word and Definition Cards for Lesson 3 are on pages 89 and 90 of the Teacher Guide.

VOCABULARY STRATEGY: Context Clues

Review with students the type of context clue in which the author provides the definition of the unknown word, usually using signal words such as "is," "are," or "is called." Have students read the first paragraph of the lesson. Have them locate the words *weather* and *climate*. Point out the context clue "is" following the word *weather* and the words "is called" preceding the word *climate*. Explain how the context clues connect the words to their meanings. As students read, tell them to underline sentences that provide definition context clues and draw an arrow to the word being defined.

LESSON 3

weather	season	desert	environment
climate	region	natural resources	recycle

Some places get rain every day. Other places are hot all year long. Other places get lots of snow. Read about why this happens.

People and the Environment

Weather

Look out a window. What can you tell about the weather? The **weather** is what the air is like outside. Weather changes all the time. Each place has its own weather. The kind of weather a place has over a long time is called **climate**.

What special clothes do you wear in rainy weather?

Seasons

A **season** is a time of year. There are four seasons each year. They are winter, spring, summer, and fall. In most places, the weather changes with the season.

 16 People and the Environment

Regions

A **region** is an area that shares some features. Joe lives in the Southwest. In this region, much of the land is dry. Little rain falls. It is a **desert**.

Why is this a good house for the desert?

We Need the Earth

Nature is full of things that people can use. These things are **natural resources**. They include water, air, and sunlight. They include plants and soil, too. They are all part of our environment. The **environment** is the natural world around you.

Plants and animals are natural resources.

Keeping the Earth Safe

We must use natural resources wisely. One way to do that is to recycle. When we **recycle**, we change something so it can be used again. Old cans are made into new cans. Old glass is used to make roads.

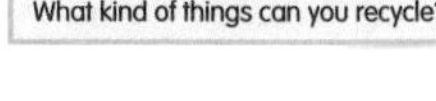

What kind of things can you recycle?

My Social Studies Words

Go to page 77 to list the other words you have learned about people and the environment.

People and the Environment 17 

DURING READING 

Read the selection aloud to students as they follow along in their books, pausing at the end of each paragraph or section. Review any words or concepts that students are having trouble with. Remind students that there is a glossary at the back of the student book that contains all of the words that appear in boldfaced type in the lesson.

- Read the caption for the picture at the bottom of page 16, "What special clothes do you wear in rainy weather?" Ask students what special clothes the children in the picture are wearing (*boots, raincoats, an umbrella*).
- Direct students' attention to the picture at the top of page 17. Read the caption aloud. Discuss why this house is a good house for the desert. (*It is made of materials found in the desert. It has plants that don't need a lot of water. It is cool because the sun doesn't shine directly inside.*)
- Remind students that the environment is the natural world around us. Reinforce the meaning of *environment* by asking questions such as these: Are trees part of the environment? Is our school part of the environment? Are flowers part of the environment? Are cars part of the environment?
- Discuss the value of recycling. Have student name items or materials that can be recycled.

Have students read the passage again on their own.

AFTER READING

Review Graphic Organizer 

Answer any questions students have about the reading selection. Then have students complete or review their graphic organizer and share it with the class.

My Social Studies Words 

Encourage students to turn to My Social Studies Words on page 77 of the student book and use the space provided to add other words about the weather and the environment.

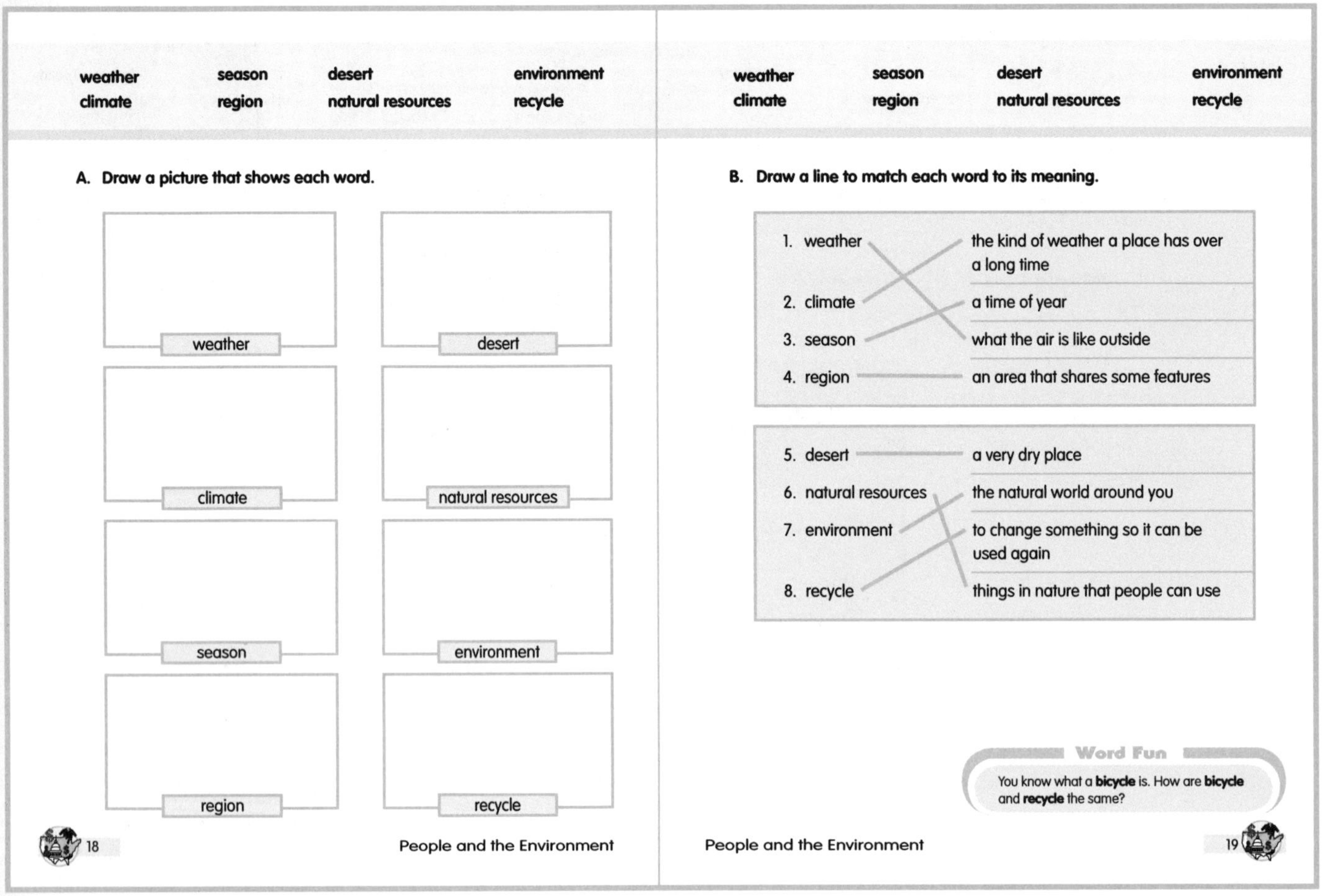

weather	season	desert	environment
climate	region	natural resources	recycle

A. Draw a picture that shows each word.

weather
desert
climate
natural resources
season
environment
region
recycle

weather	season	desert	environment
climate	region	natural resources	recycle

B. Draw a line to match each word to its meaning.

1. weather	the kind of weather a place has over a long time
2. climate	a time of year
3. season	what the air is like outside
4. region	an area that shares some features

5. desert	a very dry place
6. natural resources	the natural world around you
7. environment	to change something so it can be used again
8. recycle	things in nature that people can use

Word Fun

You know what a **bicycle** is. How are **bicycle** and **recycle** the same?

ACTIVITIES A–C

Encourage students to complete as many of the activities as possible. Remind students that they may refer to the Glossary at the back of their book as they complete the activities. Students may work independently, in small groups, or as a class. When students are done, discuss the answers for each activity.

Extensions 

These extension ideas allow you to reuse or expand upon the activities. Share them with students who complete the activities before other students, or have students do them for additional practice with target vocabulary words.

A Find the target vocabulary word that begins with the prefix *re-*, meaning "again" (*recycle*). List other words that begin with that prefix (*reread, redo, rewrite, replace, revisit*).

B Choose a target vocabulary word and write a question that includes that word.

C Choose one target vocabulary word. Write a sentence that includes that word. Then draw a picture that illustrates your sentence.

WORD FUN

Write the word *bicycle* on the board and circle the word part *cycle*. Have students think about what happens "again and again" on a bicycle.

weather climate season region desert natural resources environment recycle

C. Use a word from above to finish each sentence.

1. Not many plants can grow in the ___desert___.
2. Air, sunlight, and water are ___natural resources___ that people use.
3. To use something again and again is to ___recycle___ it.
4. The weather in Florida is usually hot. Florida has a hot ___climate___.
5. On a winter day, the ___weather___ can be snowy.
6. All the things in the natural world around you make up your ___environment___.
7. Summer is one ___season___ of the year.
8. The Southwest is a ___region___ with a desert.

weather climate season region desert natural resources environment recycle

Write!

What is the climate like where you live? Do you have seasons? What weather do you get in each season? Tell about your region.

Answers will vary. See sample answer.

Write!

Provide each student with a copy of Writing Graphic Organizer: Details Cube on Teacher Guide page 72 to use before they start writing. Students should write the season names *spring, summer, winter, fall* in the four spaces. Then they should add words they plan to use to write about each season.

Sample Answer

The climate around me is cold in the winter. It is hot in the summer. My region has four seasons. Each one is different. In the winter, we get snow. In the summer, it is dry and sunny. In the fall, the weather is cool. The leaves fall. In the spring, it is rainy.

TAKE-HOME ACTIVITY

Assign the Take-Home Activity to students for additional practice with the target vocabulary words. The reproducible Take-Home Activity for Lesson 3 is on page 75 of the Teacher Guide.

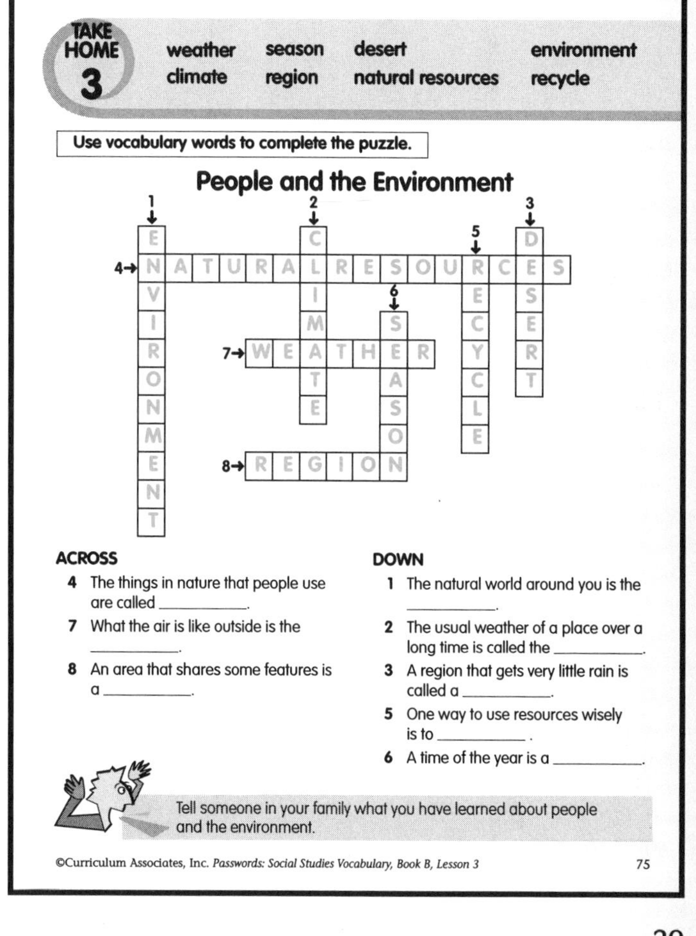

TAKE HOME 3

weather climate season region desert natural resources environment recycle

Use vocabulary words to complete the puzzle.

People and the Environment

ACROSS

4 The things in nature that people use are called ________.

7 What the air is like outside is the ________.

8 An area that shares some features is a ________.

DOWN

1 The natural world around you is the ________.

2 The usual weather of a place over a long time is called the ________.

3 A region that gets very little rain is called a ________.

5 One way to use resources wisely is to ________.

6 A time of the year is a ________.

Tell someone in your family what you have learned about people and the environment.

LESSON 4 Good Citizens

(Student Book pages 22–27)

Lesson Summary A citizen is a person who belongs to a place. Citizens have rights and responsibilities. Voting, following rules, and obeying laws are all responsibilities of citizens. Citizens who don't obey the law are brought before a judge.

TARGET VOCABULARY

citizen a person who belongs to a place

right something you are free to do

citizenship good behavior as a citizen

responsibility something you should do

vote show what you are for or against

rule something that tells people what they should or should not do

law a rule that everyone must follow

judge a person who decides the best way to follow the laws

COGNATES

Spanish-speaking students may find a discussion of the similarities and differences between English and Spanish cognates helpful.

English	Spanish
responsibility	responsabilidad
vote	voto
rule	regla
law	ley
judge	juez

BEFORE READING

Activate Prior Knowledge 

Read aloud the title of the lesson and the first sentence of the lesson that defines *citizen.* Write the word *citizen* in the center of a concept web. Ask students to tell what they know about citizens of the United States. Record their ideas in the web. Save the web and return to it after students complete the lesson so they can add details they have learned about citizens.

Introduce Target Vocabulary 

Tell students they are about to read a selection about good citizens. Write the target vocabulary words on the board. Model the pronunciation of each word and have student volunteers repeat the word. Discuss the meaning of each word and, if necessary, write the definition next to the word.

Present Graphic Organizer 

Provide each student with a copy of Vocabulary Graphic Organizer: Word Web, Teacher Guide page 68. Assign each student a target vocabulary word. Have students write the word in the center circle of the web. In the surrounding circles, have students write the word's definition, a sentence from the lesson that includes the word, an original sentence using the word, and a word they associate with the target vocabulary word.

Word and Definition Cards for Lesson 4 are on pages 91 and 92 of the Teacher Guide.

VOCABULARY STRATEGY: Print Features

Point out the heading *Doing Good Work* on page 22 of the lesson. Tell students that this is called a *heading.* Explain that headings tell the main idea of the information in the paragraphs that follow the heading. Ask students to find the headings on page 23 (*Responsibilities, Following Laws*). Then ask them to predict what the paragraphs under each heading will be about.

LESSON 4

citizen	citizenship	vote	law
right	responsibility	rule	judge

Many people live in our country. People work to make our country a good place to live. Read to learn about the work they do.

Good Citizens

Rights

A **citizen** is a person who belongs to a place. Citizens have rights. A **right** is something you are free to do. You can speak freely. You can pray where you want. You are free to live where you want.

Citizens have the right to pray where they want.

Doing Good Work

Ed was born in this country. He is a citizen. Ed helps other people. He helps clean the park. He does not throw his trash on the street. These acts show his good **citizenship**. They show he cares about people and the place where he lives.

Keeping your community clean shows good citizenship.

22 Good Citizens

Responsibilities

Citizens have responsibilities. A **responsibility** is something you should do. When you are older, you should vote. When you **vote**, you show what you are for or against.

Citizens must also follow the rules. A **rule** tells people what they should or should not do.

Yes

No

Older citizens have the responsibility to vote.

Following Laws

The rules of a place are called laws. A **law** is a rule that everyone must follow.

A person who breaks a law must see a judge. A **judge** decides the best way to follow laws. A judge also decides what a person must do to make up for breaking a law.

A law says cars must stop at a stop sign.

Judges must know the laws.

My Social Studies Words

Go to page 77 to list the other words you have learned about good citizens.

Good Citizens 23

DURING READING

Read the selection aloud to students as they follow along in their books, pausing at the end of each paragraph or section. Review any words or concepts that students are having trouble with. Remind students that there is a glossary at the back of the student book that contains all of the words that appear in boldfaced type in the lesson.

- Have students study the picture at the bottom of page 22. Ask students these questions: What is Ed doing that shows he's a good citizen? Why is cleaning the park an example of good citizenship?
- Write the word *responsibility* on the board. Circle each syllable. Help students pronounce the word as they clap the syllables. Then have students say the word and use it in a sentence.
- Use the illustration of the stop sign on page 23 to begin a discussion about laws. Ask students to talk about any laws they are aware of.
- Discuss the difference between a rule and a law. Discuss the consequences of breaking each one. Make a two-column chart with the headings *Rules* and *Laws*. Ask students to give examples of rules and laws and record their ideas in the chart.

Have students read the passage again on their own.

AFTER READING

Review Graphic Organizer

Answer any questions students have about the reading selection. Then have students complete or review their graphic organizer and share it with the class.

My Social Studies Words

Encourage students to turn to My Social Studies Words on page 77 of the student book and use the space provided to add other words about good citizens.

citizen	**citizenship**	**vote**	**law**
right	**responsibility**	**rule**	**judge**

A. Circle the word that goes with each picture.

1. law / judge / (right)
2. (law) / vote / citizen
3. rule / (citizen) / vote
4. right / citizen / (vote)
5. vote / (judge) / citizenship
6. vote / (rule) / citizen
7. right / judge / (citizenship)
8. right / vote / (responsibility)

STOP

POOL RULES
- WALK
- DON'T RUN
- WEAR SWIMCAPS
- NO RUNNING

☑ Yes
☐ No

24 Good Citizens

citizen	**citizenship**	**vote**	**law**
right	**responsibility**	**rule**	**judge**

B. Circle the word that answers each riddle.

What Am I?

1. I am the way you show what you are for or against.
   judge rule (vote)
2. I am something that tells what you should or should not do.
   judge vote (rule)
3. I am a person who belongs to a place.
   right (citizen) law
4. I am a person who decides the best way to follow laws.
   (judge) law responsibility
5. I am a rule that everyone must follow.
   right (law) judge
6. I am a way of showing that I care about the place where I live.
   (citizenship) vote right
7. I am something you are free to do.
   (right) judge law
8. I am something you should do.
   citizen judge (responsibility)

Word Fun

The word **right** also means "not wrong." It can also mean "not left."

Good Citizens 25

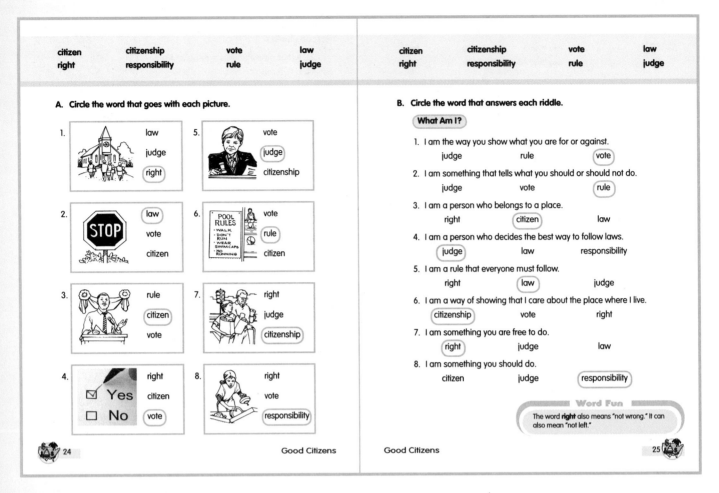

ACTIVITIES A–C

Encourage students to complete as many of the activities as possible. Remind students that they may refer to the Glossary at the back of their book as they complete the activities. Students may work independently, in small groups, or as a class. When students are done, discuss the answers for each activity.

Extensions 

These extension ideas allow you to reuse or expand upon the activities. Share them with students who complete the activities before other students, or have students do them for additional practice with target vocabulary words.

A Find and write the three target vocabulary words that have more than one syllable. Draw a line between the syllables in the words.

B Choose one target vocabulary word and write as many words as you can think of that rhyme with it.

C Write a sentence about a rule that you have to follow in school or at home. Draw a picture of yourself following that rule.

WORD FUN

Review the three different meanings of *right*. Then say sentences such as the ones below. Tell students to give a "thumbs up" every time they hear a sentence that uses the word *right* to mean "something you are free to do."

- Turn right at the bottom of the hill.
- You have a right to speak freely.
- Carlos knew he had the right answer.

citizen	citizenship	vote	law
right	responsibility	rule	judge

C. Use a word from above to finish each sentence.

1. To show good ___citizenship___, help keep your community clean.
2. All drivers must follow the ___law___ and stop at red lights.
3. The pool has a ___rule___ against running.
4. You have the ___right___ to speak freely.
5. It is my ___responsibility___ to set the table for dinner.
6. If someone breaks a law, a ___judge___ might send that person to jail.
7. You tell what you are for or against when you ___vote___.
8. You are a ___citizen___ of the place where you live.

26 Good Citizens

citizen	citizenship	vote	law
right	responsibility	rule	judge

Write!

Tell what responsibility you have at your home. How does it help your family?

Answers will vary. See sample answer.

Good Citizens 27

Write!

Provide each student with a copy of Writing Graphic Organizer: Details Cube on Teacher Guide page 72, to use before they start writing. Tell students to read the question carefully, then think about what they want to say in their answers. Tell students to write words or phrases in three or four boxes of the cube. Explain that these words and phrases will be the details they include in their answers. When students are ready to begin writing, provide a sentence starter such as the following: *At home, my responsibility is ________.*

Sample Answer

At home, my responsibility is to clean my room. I pick up my clothes and put them away. This helps my family because it keeps our house clean. When I clean up, I make my mom happy.

TAKE-HOME ACTIVITY

Assign the Take-Home Activity to students for additional practice with the target vocabulary words. The reproducible Take-Home Activity for Lesson 4 is on page 76 of the Teacher Guide.

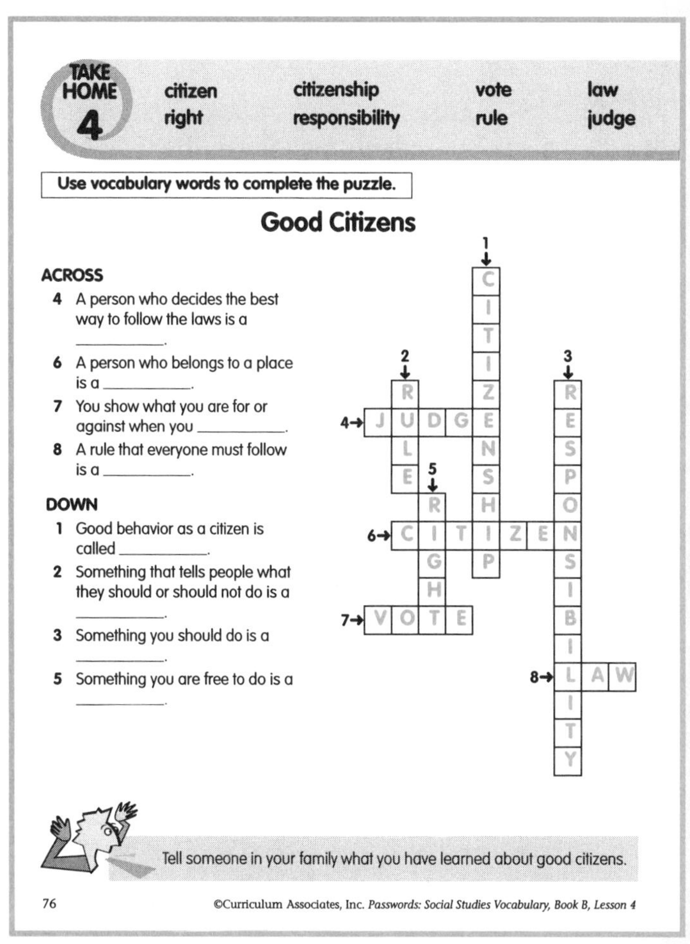
TAKE HOME 4

citizen	citizenship	vote	law
right	responsibility	rule	judge

Use vocabulary words to complete the puzzle.

Good Citizens

ACROSS

4 A person who decides the best way to follow the laws is a ________.

6 A person who belongs to a place is a ________.

7 You show what you are for or against when you ________.

8 A rule that everyone must follow is a ________.

DOWN

1 Good behavior as a citizen is called ________.

2 Something that tells people what they should or should not do is a ________.

3 Something you should do is a ________.

5 Something you are free to do is a ________.

Tell someone in your family what you have learned about good citizens.

76 ©Curriculum Associates, Inc. *Passwords: Social Studies Vocabulary, Book B, Lesson 4*

LESSON 5

Government

(Student Book pages 28–33)

Lesson Summary Local government runs a town or a city. Most local governments are led by a mayor who is helped by a city council. A state government is led by a governor. Citizens pay taxes to pay for the needs of communities.

TARGET VOCABULARY

government people who work together to run a city or town, a state, or the country

local government people who work together to run a town or a city

leader a person who leads others

election the time when we vote for our leaders

mayor the leader of a town

city council the people who help the mayor lead a town

governor the leader of a state

tax money from citizens that pays for the needs of a community

COGNATES

Spanish-speaking students may find a discussion of the similarities and differences between English and Spanish cognates helpful.

English	Spanish
government	gobierno
leader	líder
election	elección
governor	gobernador

BEFORE READING

Activate Prior Knowledge 

Read aloud the introductory paragraph above the lesson title. Ask students to suggest possible answers to the question. List their ideas on the board. Return to the list after students have completed the lesson.

Introduce Target Vocabulary  

Tell students they are about to read a selection about our government. Write the target vocabulary words on the board. Model the pronunciation of each word and have student volunteers repeat the word. Discuss the meaning of each word and, if necessary, write the definition next to the word.

Present Graphic Organizer 

Provide each student with a copy of Vocabulary Graphic Organizer: Knowledge Scale, Teacher Guide page 69. Have students write each target vocabulary word in the first column. Then tell them to put a check mark in the column that best identifies their understanding of each word. Have them write the definition of each word as they learn it in the lesson.

Word and Definition Cards for Lesson 5 are on pages 93 and 94 of the Teacher Guide.

VOCABULARY STRATEGY: Suffixes

Remind students that a suffix is a group of letters that is added to the end of a word. Write the target vocabulary words *leader* and *governor* on the board and circle the suffixes *-er* and *-or*. Tell students that these two suffixes have the same meaning. Ask them if, based on those words, they can tell what the suffixes *-er* and *-or* mean. If necessary, provide additional examples such as *swimmer, teacher, actor,* and *conductor*. Lead them to understand that both suffixes mean "a person who." Explain that a *leader* is a person who leads, and a *governor* is a person who governs. You may want to point out the word *mayor* and explain that the letters *or* at the end of *mayor* are not a suffix.

LESSON 5

government **local government** **leader** **election** **mayor** **city council** **governor** **tax**

A community cannot run without help. People must be put in charge. Who are these people? What do they do? Read to find out.

Government

The **government** is made of people who work for the good of all. There are three types of governments. A **local government** runs a town or city. A state government runs the state. The biggest government of all runs the whole country.

Local government meets at a town hall.

Finding Leaders

The people in a place choose their leaders. A **leader** is a person who leads others. People vote to choose a leader. An **election** is a time when we vote for our leaders. The person with the most votes wins.

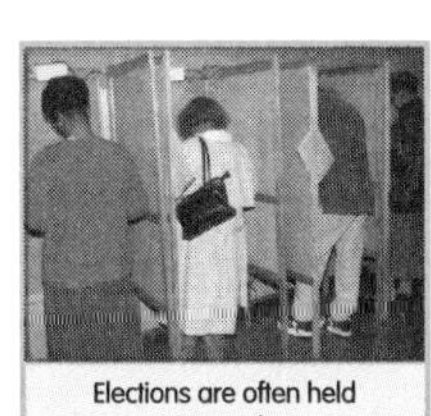
Elections are often held in November.

The Leader of a Town or City

A **mayor** is the leader of a town or city. Some mayors have many people to help with the job. They make up the **city council**. They listen to the citizens. They find ways to help them.

Who is your mayor?

The Leader of a State

A **governor** is the leader of a state. The governor works to help the people in that state.

Paying for a Community's Needs

Towns and cities have many needs. They need good roads. They need schools. They need police. The government tries to meet those needs. They use taxes to pay for the needs. A **tax** is money paid by citizens and businesses. Taxes pay for roads. They pay for schools and police.

A governor has many responsibilities.

My Social Studies Words

Go to page 78 to list the other words you have learned about government.

DURING READING 

Read the selection aloud to students as they follow along in their books, pausing at the end of each paragraph or section. Review any words or concepts that students are having trouble with. Remind students that there is a glossary at the back of the student book that contains all of the words that appear in boldfaced type in the lesson.

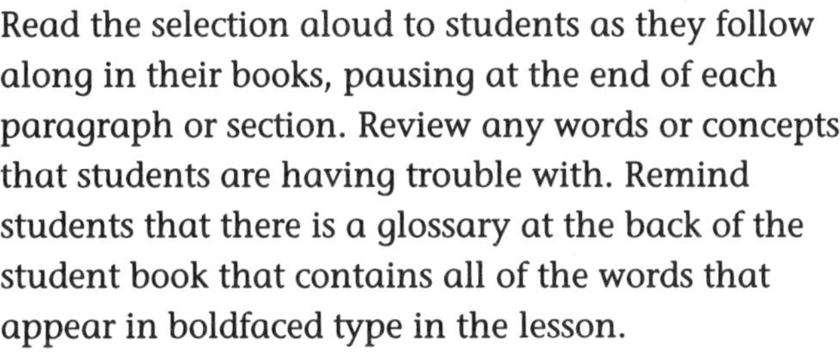

- Have students follow along as you read the first paragraph of the lesson. Point out the words *run* and *runs* in several sentences. Because students may be unfamiliar with this meaning of the word, explain that *run* can mean "to operate or make something work," such as "run a washing machine." Explain that a government makes a city work. A government makes a state work.
- Have students read the caption under the illustration at the top of page 28. Ask students if they know where their local government meets.
- Read the captions under the pictures on page 29 aloud to students. Tell students the name of their mayor and governor if they do not know.
- In addition to schools and libraries, ask students to name other community needs that are paid for with tax money. Guide them to think about expenses associated with things such as roads, parks, water, and sports programs.

Have students read the passage again on their own.

AFTER READING

Review Graphic Organizer 

Answer any questions students have about the reading selection. Then have students complete or review their graphic organizer and share it with the class.

My Social Studies Words 

Encourage students to turn to My Social Studies Words on page 78 of the student book and use the space provided to add other words about government.

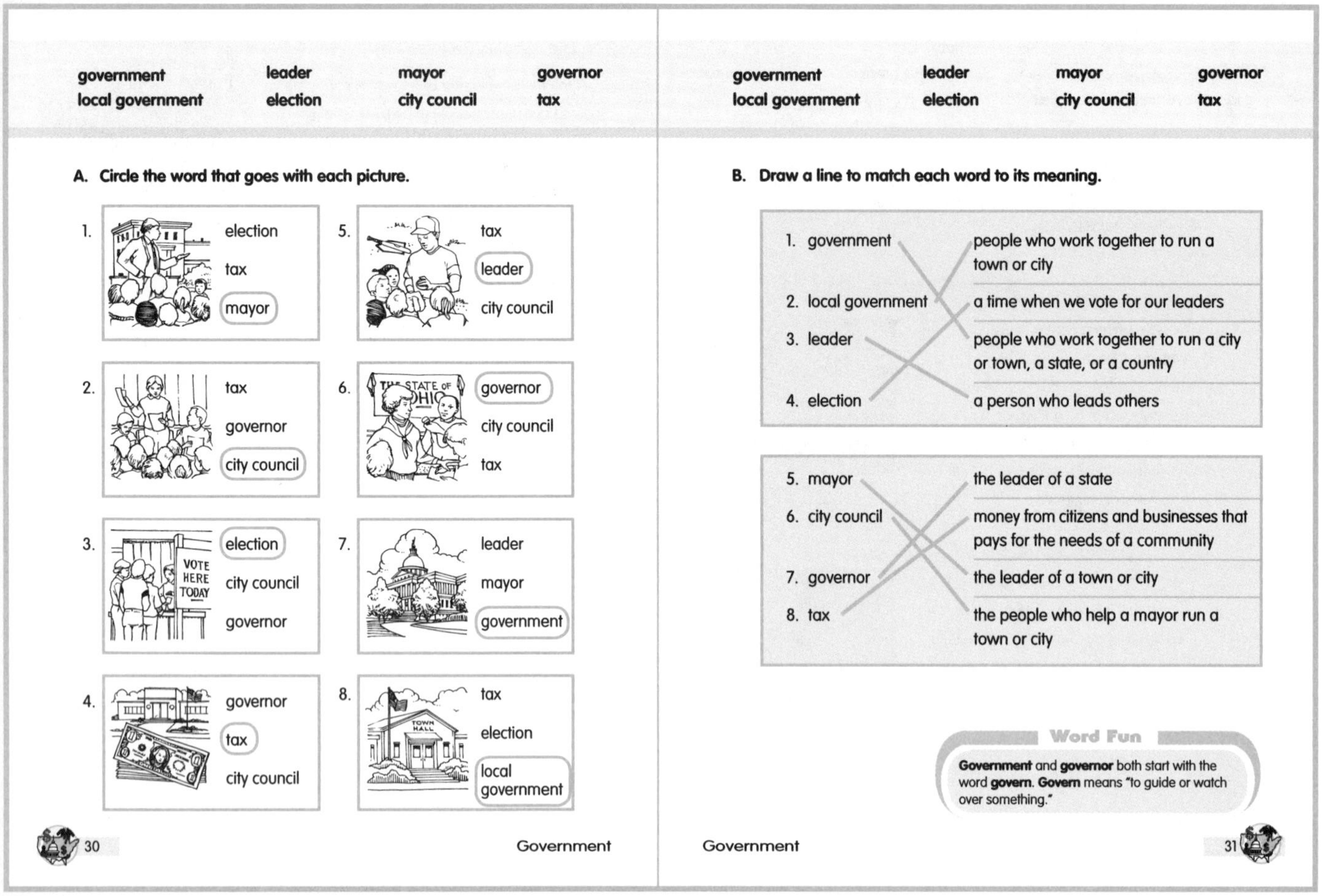

government	leader	mayor	governor
local government	election	city council	tax

A. Circle the word that goes with each picture.

1. election / tax / mayor
2. tax / governor / city council
3. election / city council / governor
4. governor / tax / city council
5. tax / leader / city council
6. governor / city council / tax
7. leader / mayor / government
8. tax / election / local government

30 Government

government	leader	mayor	governor
local government	election	city council	tax

B. Draw a line to match each word to its meaning.

1. government	people who work together to run a town or city
2. local government	a time when we vote for our leaders
3. leader	people who work together to run a city or town, a state, or a country
4. election	a person who leads others

5. mayor	the leader of a state
6. city council	money from citizens and businesses that pays for the needs of a community
7. governor	the leader of a town or city
8. tax	the people who help a mayor run a town or city

Word Fun

Government and **governor** both start with the word **govern**. **Govern** means "to guide or watch over something."

Government 31

ACTIVITIES A–C

Encourage students to complete as many of the activities as possible. Remind students that they may refer to the Glossary at the back of their book as they complete the activities. Students may work independently, in small groups, or as a class. When students are done, discuss the answers for each activity.

Extensions 

These extension ideas allow you to reuse or expand upon the activities. Share them with students who complete the activities before other students, or have students do them for additional practice with target vocabulary words.

A Draw lines between the syllables of each target vocabulary word.

B Choose one of the sentences you completed in Activity C. Draw a picture to illustrate the sentence.

C Choose one target vocabulary word. Write a question that includes that word. Then write the answer to your question.

WORD FUN

Explain to students that many English words come from other languages. Many of them come from old languages, such as Greek and Latin. Tell students that the word *government* comes from a Greek word that means "to steer." Ask them to share ideas about how a government and steering a car might be similar.

government	leader	mayor	governor
local government	election	city council	tax

C. Use a word from above to finish each sentence.

1. People in the state voted for a new governor.
2. The people on the city council help the mayor.
3. Each family and business pays a tax. It helps pay for the needs of the community.
4. The people who work together to run our country are our government.
5. A governor is a state's leader.
6. People who run a town or city are part of local government.
7. The people in a state vote for their leaders in an election.
8. The leader of a city government is the mayor.

32 Government

government	leader	mayor	governor
local government	election	city council	tax

Write!

Think about the leaders you know. You have a leader in your school. Maybe you are on a team with a leader. Tell about one leader you know. What does that person do to be a good leader?

Answers will vary. See sample answer.

Government 33

Write!

Provide each student with a copy of Writing Graphic Organizer: Web on Teacher Guide page 71, to use before they start writing. Students should write the name of the leader they have in mind in the center circle. In the surrounding circles, they should write words and phrases that tell why that person is a good leader.

Sample Answer

Mrs. Cho is the leader of my scout troop. She is a good leader. She teaches us how to tie knots in ropes. She takes us camping. She shows us how to cook food over a campfire. She plays games with us.

TAKE-HOME ACTIVITY

Assign the Take-Home Activity to students for additional practice with the target vocabulary words. The reproducible Take-Home Activity for Lesson 5 is on page 77 of the Teacher Guide.

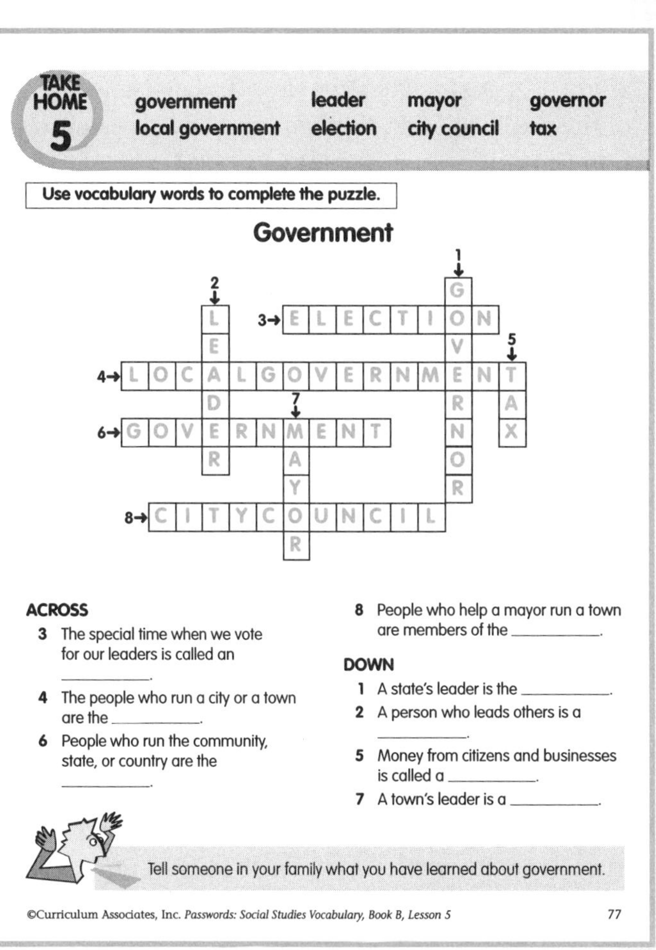

TAKE HOME 5

government	leader	mayor	governor
local government	election	city council	tax

Use vocabulary words to complete the puzzle.

Government

ACROSS

3 The special time when we vote for our leaders is called an ______.

4 The people who run a city or a town are the ______.

6 People who run the community, state, or country are the ______.

8 People who help a mayor run a town are members of the ______.

DOWN

1 A state's leader is the ______.

2 A person who leads others is a ______.

5 Money from citizens and businesses is called a ______.

7 A town's leader is a ______.

Tell someone in your family what you have learned about government.

 77

LESSON 6 Our Nation's Government

(Student Book pages 34–39)

Lesson Summary Our nation's government is made of three branches. The branch that makes laws is the Congress. Congress meets in the Capitol. The president is part of another branch. The president lives in the White House. The third branch is the Supreme Court. It makes sure that people follow the Constitution.

TARGET VOCABULARY

nation another word for country

branches parts of the government

Congress the part of the government that makes laws

Capitol the building where Congress works

president the leader of our nation

White House the home of the President

Supreme Court the part of the government that makes sure the laws are fair

Constitution the law of the land

COGNATES

Spanish-speaking students may find a discussion of the similarities and differences between English and Spanish cognates helpful.

English	Spanish
nation	nación
Congress	Congreso
Capitol	Capitolio
president	presidente
Constitution	Constitución

BEFORE READING

Activate Prior Knowledge 

Read aloud the introductory paragraph above the lesson title. Ask students to suggest possible answers to the question. List their ideas on the board. Return to the list after students have completed the lesson.

Introduce Target Vocabulary  

Tell students they are about to read a selection about our country's government. Write the target vocabulary words on the board. Model the pronunciation of each word and have student volunteers repeat the word. Discuss the meaning of each word and, if necessary, write the definition next to the word.

Present Graphic Organizer 

Provide each student with a copy of Vocabulary Graphic Organizer: Word Web, Teacher Guide page 68. Assign each student a target vocabulary word. Have students write the word in the center circle of the web. In the surrounding circles, have students write the word's definition, a sentence from the lesson that includes the word, an original sentence using the word, and a word they associate with the target vocabulary word.

Word and Definition Cards for Lesson 6 are on pages 95 and 96 of the Teacher Guide.

VOCABULARY STRATEGY: Homophones

Explain to students that some words sound the same, but they have different spellings and different meanings. Write the target vocabulary word *Capitol* on the board and pronounce it. Explain that the *Capitol* is an important building in Washington, D.C. It's where Congress works. Then write the word *capital* on the board and pronounce it. Write the letters A, B, and C on the board. Point out to students that these are *capital* letters. Say sentences such as those that follow. Have volunteers come to the board and point to the word that is in each sentence. *My name begins with a capital letter. Congress works in the Capitol building. Every sentence begins with a capital letter. A flag flies over the Capitol building.*

LESSON 6

nation **branches** **Congress** **Capitol** **president** **White House** **Supreme Court** **Constitution**

Local government runs a city. State government runs a state. What is the government of our country? Keep reading to find out.

Our Nation's Government

We live in the United States. It is our **nation**, or country. Our nation has a government. It is in Washington, D.C.

Congress

The government has three **branches**, or parts. One branch is called Congress. **Congress** makes the laws for our country. Each state sends people to be part of Congress. They speak for their state. They meet and work in the **Capitol**.

The Capitol is in Washington, D.C.

The President

The leader of our nation is the **president**. The president makes up another branch of the government. The president lives and works in the **White House**.

Many people visit the White House every year.

The Supreme Court

The third branch of government is the **Supreme Court**. It is the highest court in the nation. Nine judges make up this court. They make sure that all of us follow the **Constitution**. It is the law of our nation.

Supreme Court judges work in this building.

The Constitution was written over 200 years ago.

My Social Studies Words

Go to page 78 to list the other words you have learned about our nation's government.

DURING READING

Read the selection aloud to students as they follow along in their books, pausing at the end of each paragraph or section. Review any words or concepts that students are having trouble with. Remind students that there is a glossary at the back of the student book that contains all of the words that appear in boldfaced type in the lesson.

- Direct students' attention to the map on page 34. Help students to locate their state on the map and color it. Discuss with students the distance between their state and Washington, D.C. Is it close or far? How would they get to Washington, D.C., if they were to visit?
- After reading the text under the heading "The President," ask students if they know the name of the current president. Write the president's name on the board.
- Point out the word *Supreme* in *Supreme Court.* Explain that *supreme* means, "the highest, or most important."
- Use the illustrations of the White House, the Capitol building, and the building that houses the Supreme Court to review information about each one. Ask students to identify each building, tell who works in each one, and tell the kind of work that takes place in each location.

Have students read the passage again on their own.

AFTER READING

Review Graphic Organizer

Answer any questions students have about the reading selection. Then have students complete or review their graphic organizer and share it with the class.

My Social Studies Words

Encourage students to turn to My Social Studies Words on page 78 of the student book and use the space provided to add other words about our nation's government.

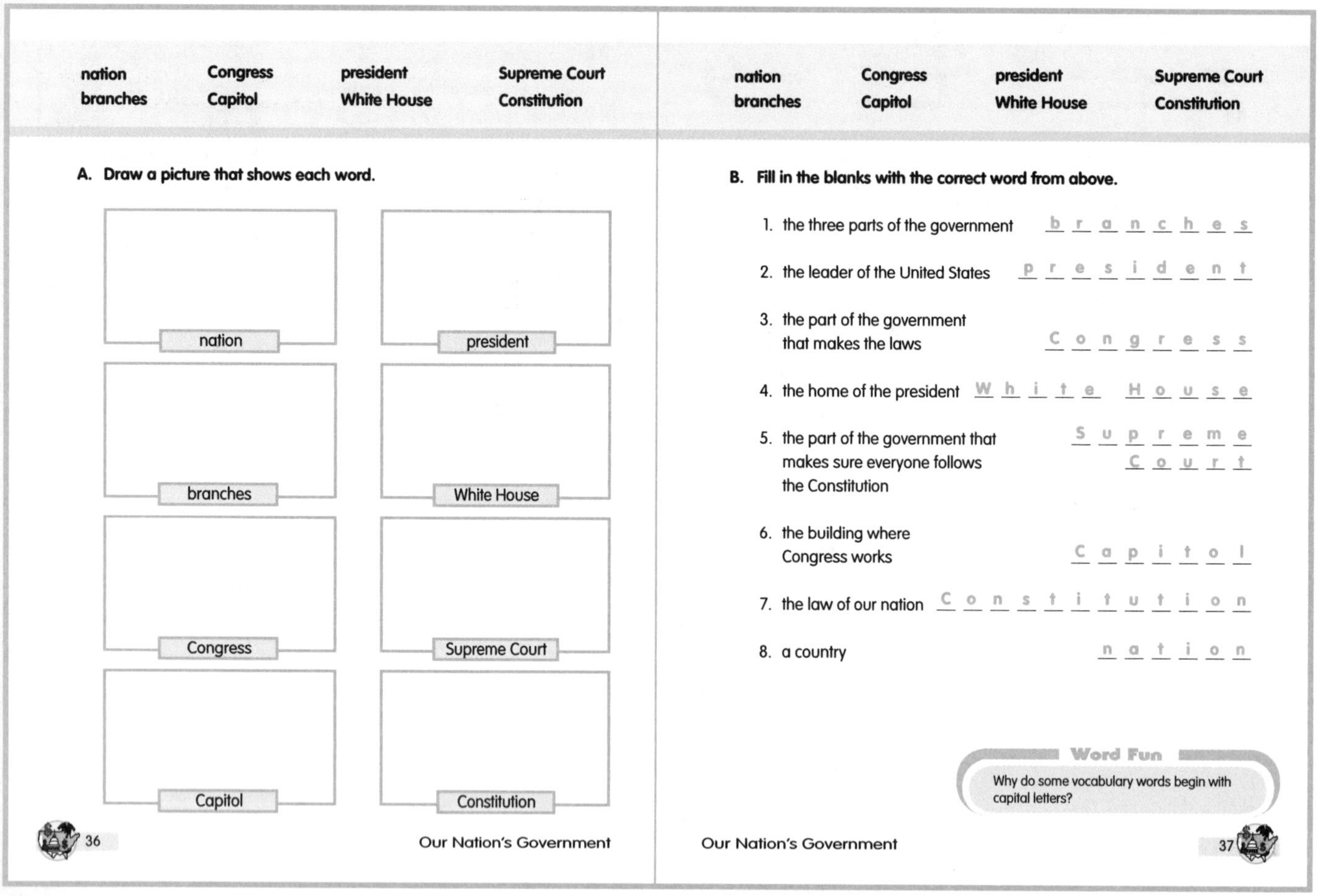

nation	Congress	president	Supreme Court
branches	Capitol	White House	Constitution

A. Draw a picture that shows each word.

nation

president

branches

White House

Congress

Supreme Court

Capitol

Constitution

36 Our Nation's Government

nation	Congress	president	Supreme Court
branches	Capitol	White House	Constitution

B. Fill in the blanks with the correct word from above.

1. the three parts of the government b r a n c h e s
2. the leader of the United States p r e s i d e n t
3. the part of the government that makes the laws C o n g r e s s
4. the home of the president W h i t e H o u s e
5. the part of the government that makes sure everyone follows the Constitution S u p r e m e C o u r t
6. the building where Congress works C a p i t o l
7. the law of our nation C o n s t i t u t i o n
8. a country n a t i o n

Word Fun

Why do some vocabulary words begin with capital letters?

Our Nation's Government 37

ACTIVITIES A–C

Encourage students to complete as many of the activities as possible. Remind students that they may refer to the Glossary at the back of their book as they complete the activities. Students may work independently, in small groups, or as a class. When students are done, discuss the answers for each activity.

Extensions

These extension ideas allow you to reuse or expand upon the activities. Share them with students who complete the activities before other students, or have students do them for additional practice with target vocabulary words.

A Write each target vocabulary word on a piece of paper. Work with a partner and take turns choosing a word, reading it, and using it in a sentence.

B Write the letters in the word *nation* in a vertical column. Try to think of things that can be found in our nation that begin with each letter in the word. Write the word next to the letter.

C Rewrite the sentences you completed in Activity C as questions.

WORD FUN

Ask students to name buildings in their own city or town, such as a school, a library, and a hospital. Write the names of the buildings without capital letters, then have volunteers rewrite the names to show the correct capitalization.

nation	Congress	president	Supreme Court
branches	Capitol	White House	Constitution

C. Use a word from above to finish each sentence.

1. I heard a speech by the ___president___ of the United States.
2. The president lives and works in the ___White House___.
3. If you were a member of Congress, you would work in the ___Capitol___.
4. Nine judges make up the ___Supreme Court___.
5. Congress, the president, and the Supreme Court make up three ___branches___ of our government.
6. A law gets made by the people in ___Congress___.
7. A country with its own government is called a ___nation___.
8. Everyone in our country must follow the ___Constitution___.

38 Our Nation's Government

nation	Congress	president	Supreme Court
branches	Capitol	White House	Constitution

Write!

Who is the president of the United States? Tell what the president does for the nation.

Answers will vary. See sample answer.

Our Nation's Government 39

Write!

Provide each student with a copy of Writing Graphic Organizer: Web on Teacher Guide page 71, to use before they start writing. Students should write the president's name in the center circle. In the surrounding circles, they should write words and phrases that tell about what the president does. If necessary, provide a sentence starter such as, *The president of the United States is _______.*

Sample Answer

The president of the United States is George Bush. He helps decide how to keep our nation safe. He makes sure people follow the rules of the country.

TAKE-HOME ACTIVITY

Assign the Take-Home Activity to students for additional practice with the target vocabulary words. The reproducible Take-Home Activity for Lesson 6 is on page 78 of the Teacher Guide.

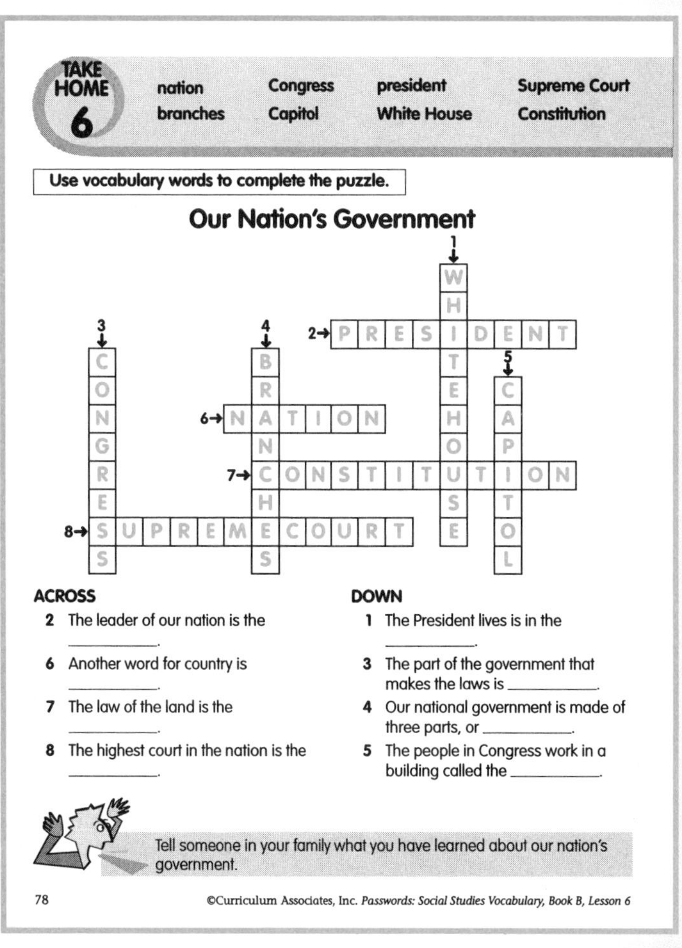

TAKE HOME 6

nation	Congress	president	Supreme Court
branches	Capitol	White House	Constitution

Use vocabulary words to complete the puzzle.

Our Nation's Government

ACROSS

2 The leader of our nation is the _______.

6 Another word for country is _______.

7 The law of the land is the _______.

8 The highest court in the nation is the _______.

DOWN

1 The President lives is in the _______.

3 The part of the government that makes the laws is _______.

4 Our national government is made of three parts, or _______.

5 The people in Congress work in a building called the _______.

Tell someone in your family what you have learned about our nation's government.

78

LESSON 7 Work and Money

(Student Book pages 40–45)

Lesson Summary People have both wants and needs. Wants are the things people would like to have, and needs are the things they must have to live. People buy the things they want and need with income from their jobs. In order to save money to buy the things they want, people put money in savings accounts in banks.

TARGET VOCABULARY

goods things that are made or grown

market a place to buy and sell things

price the amount of money you pay to buy something

needs things that people must have to live

wants things that people would like to have

income the money people get from work

services jobs people do to help other people

savings account a place to put money in a bank

COGNATES

Spanish-speaking students may find a discussion of the similarities and differences between English and Spanish cognates helpful.

English	Spanish
market	mercado
price	precio
services	servicios

BEFORE READING

Activate Prior Knowledge  

Introduce the target vocabulary words *wants* and *needs* at this point. Create a two-column chart on the board and label the columns *Wants* and *Needs.* Ask students to name examples of wants and needs and record their suggestions in the chart. After students read the lesson, return to the chart and use it to generate questions about goods and money.

Introduce Target Vocabulary  

Tell students they are about to read a selection about money and the things we buy with it. Write the target vocabulary words on the board. Model the pronunciation of each word and have student volunteers repeat the word. Discuss the meaning of each word and, if necessary, write the definition next to the word.

Present Graphic Organizer 

Provide each student with a copy of Vocabulary Graphic Organizer: Knowledge Scale, Teacher Guide page 69. Have students write each target vocabulary word in the first column. Then tell them to put a check mark in the column that best identifies their understanding of each word. Have them write the definition of each word as they learn it in the lesson.

Word and Definition Cards for Lesson 7 are on pages 97 and 98 of the Teacher Guide.

VOCABULARY STRATEGY: Context Clues

Review with students the type of context clue in which the author provides a definition of the unknown word, usually using signal words such as "is," "are," or "is called." Direct students' attention to the first paragraph of the lesson. Have them locate the word *goods* and the context clue "are." As students read, tell them to underline words that provide definition context clues and draw an arrow to the word being defined.

LESSON 7

goods **price** **wants** **services**
market **needs** **income** **savings account**

There are many things to buy. But you can't buy them all. How do people get money? And how do they use it? Read to find out.

Work and Money

Every day people shop for goods. **Goods** are things that are made or grown. Books, toys, and food are goods.

Using Money

David wants to buy food. He goes to a market. A **market** is a place to buy and sell things. Each thing has a price. A **price** is the amount of money you pay to buy something.

Things that people must have to live are called **needs**. Every person needs food, clothes, and a home. **Wants** are things that people would like to have. David needs to have food. He wants to have a bike. A bike is not a need.

David needs food.

David wants a bike.

40 Work and Money

Many Kinds of Work

Mia goes to work every day. The money she gets from her work is her **income**. She uses her income to buy the things she needs. She buys goods and services.

Services are jobs people do to help other people. Teachers are service workers. They help children learn. Ben is a bus driver. He helps people get across town. People pay for his service.

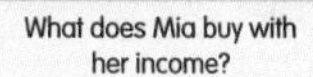

What does Mia buy with her income?

Ben's work is a service.

Keeping Money Safe

Mia and Ben cannot buy everything they want. They keep some of their income for later. They put some of it in the bank. A **savings account** is a service from a bank. It lets people keep their money safe.

Do you have a savings account?

My Social Studies Words

Go to page 79 to list the other words you have learned about work and money.

Work and Money 41

DURING READING

Read the selection aloud to students as they follow along in their books, pausing at the end of each paragraph or section. Review any words or concepts that students are having trouble with. Remind students that there is a glossary at the back of the student book that contains all of the words that appear in boldfaced type in the lesson.

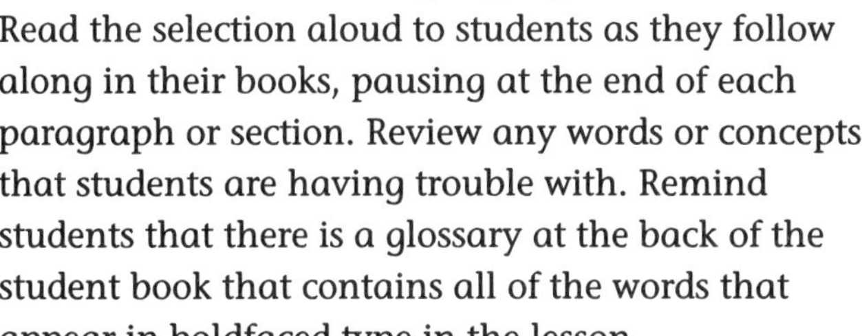

- *Wants* is a multiple-meaning word. Students will most likely be familiar with the meaning of *wants* as a verb meaning "desires." Remind them that in this lesson, *wants* is a noun meaning "things that people would like to have."
- Refer back to the chart you made to activate prior knowledge of wants and needs. See if students are ready to add other words to it.
- Use the illustration of the bus driver on page 41 as an opportunity to identify other service jobs. Guide students to think of service jobs such as librarians, mechanics, painters, police officers, firefighters, and nurses.
- Have students use the illustration of the bank on page 41 to create sentences that demonstrate their understanding of banks and savings accounts. You might want to have them complete a sentence such as this one: *If I had a savings account, I would save money to buy a* ______.

Have students read the passage again on their own.

AFTER READING

Review Graphic Organizer

Answer any questions students have about the reading selection. Then have students complete or review their graphic organizer and share it with the class.

My Social Studies Words

Encourage students to turn to My Social Studies Words on page 79 of the student book and use the space provided to add other words about work and money.

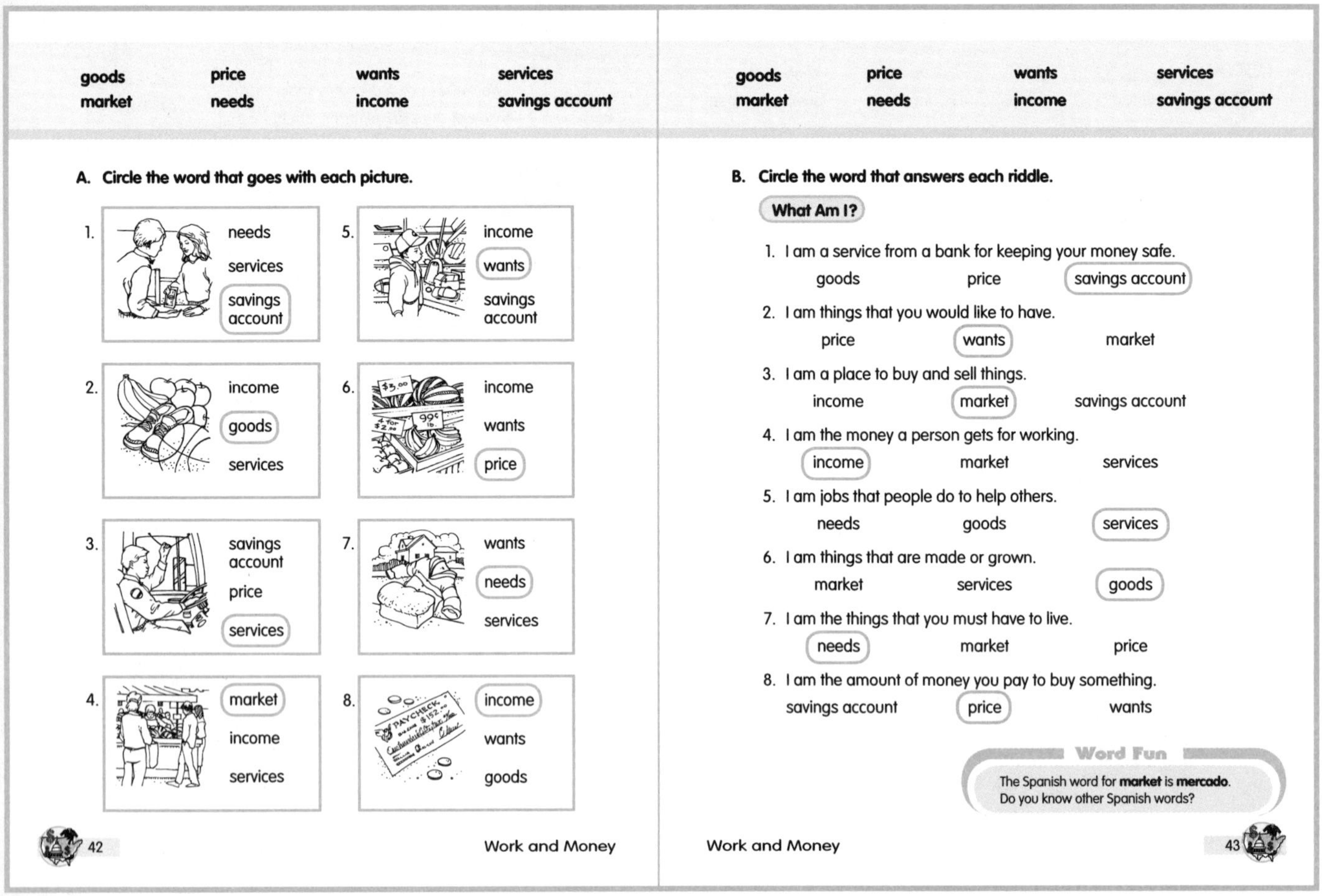

goods | price | wants | services
market | needs | income | savings account

A. Circle the word that goes with each picture.

1. needs / services / savings account
2. income / goods / services
3. savings account / price / services
4. market / income / services
5. income / wants / savings account
6. income / wants / price
7. wants / needs / services
8. income / wants / goods

42 Work and Money

goods | price | wants | services
market | needs | income | savings account

B. Circle the word that answers each riddle.

What Am I?

1. I am a service from a bank for keeping your money safe.
   goods / price / savings account
2. I am things that you would like to have.
   price / wants / market
3. I am a place to buy and sell things.
   income / market / savings account
4. I am the money a person gets for working.
   income / market / services
5. I am jobs that people do to help others.
   needs / goods / services
6. I am things that are made or grown.
   market / services / goods
7. I am the things that you must have to live.
   needs / market / price
8. I am the amount of money you pay to buy something.
   savings account / price / wants

Word Fun

The Spanish word for **market** is **mercado**. Do you know other Spanish words?

Work and Money 43

ACTIVITIES A–C

Encourage students to complete as many of the activities as possible. Remind students that they may refer to the Glossary at the back of their book as they complete the activities. Students may work independently, in small groups, or as a class. When students are done, discuss the answers for each activity.

Extensions 

These extension ideas allow you to reuse or expand upon the activities. Share them with students who complete the activities before other students, or have students do them for additional practice with target vocabulary words.

A Find the target vocabulary words that have two or more syllables. Write sentences that include those words.

B Write as many words as you can think of that rhyme with the target vocabulary word *price*.

C Draw a picture of yourself buying something in a market. Write one or two sentences that go with the picture. Use the words *market* and *price* in your sentence.

WORD FUN

Even students who think they don't know any Spanish words may know these Spanish words that are commonly used in English: *banana, cafeteria, fiesta, siesta, rodeo, taco, tornado.*

goods	price	wants	services
market	needs	income	savings account

C. Use a word from above to finish each sentence.

1. I cannot buy the shoes I want because the ___price___ is too high.
2. I put my money in a ___savings account___ at my bank.
3. I use half of my ___income___ to buy things I need.
4. A store has many ___goods___ for sale.
5. Having a place to live is one of your ___needs___.
6. Toys and games are ___wants___ because you can live without them.
7. Let's go to the ___market___ to buy some fruit.
8. Sick people pay doctors for their ___services___.

44 Work and Money

goods	price	wants	services
market	needs	income	savings account

Write!

If you could do any job, what would it be? Would you make goods? Would you do a service? Tell about the kind of work you would do.

Answers will vary. See sample answer.

Work and Money 45

Write!

Provide each student with a copy of Writing Graphic Organizer: Details Cube on Teacher Guide page 72, to use before they start writing. Tell students to read the question carefully, then think about what they want to say in their answers. Tell students to write words or phrases in three or four boxes of the cube. Explain that these words and phrases are the details they will include in their answers. When students are ready to begin writing, provide a sentence starter such as the following: *The kind of work I want to do is ________.*

Sample Answer

The kind of work I want to do is fight fires. Firefighters put out fires with big hoses. They save people. People need firefighters.

TAKE-HOME ACTIVITY

Assign the Take-Home Activity to students for additional practice with the target vocabulary words. The reproducible Take-Home Activity for Lesson 7 is on page 79 of the Teacher Guide.

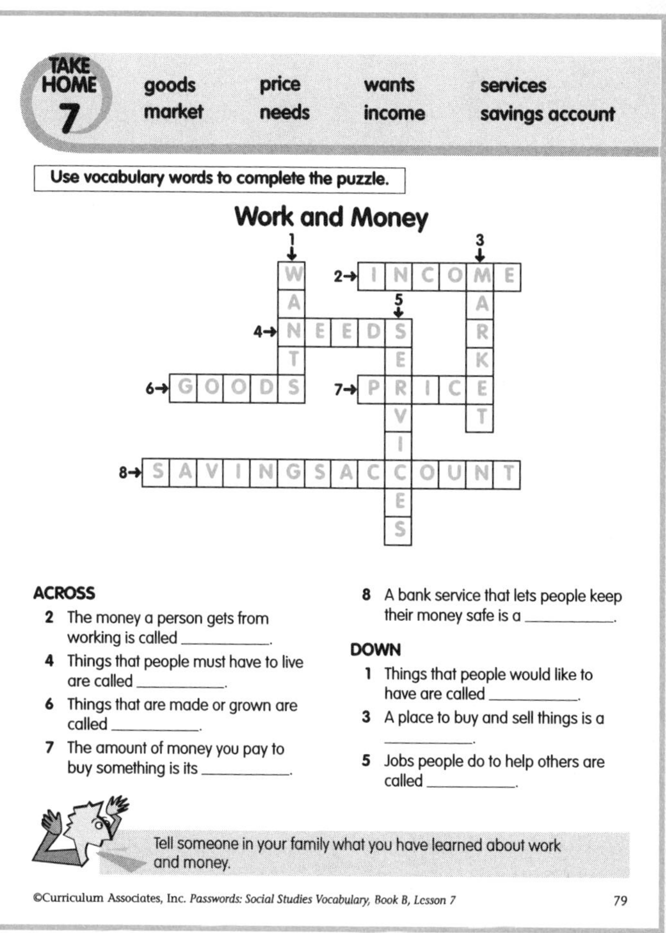

TAKE HOME 7

goods	price	wants	services
market	needs	income	savings account

Use vocabulary words to complete the puzzle.

Work and Money

ACROSS
2 The money a person gets from working is called ________. (INCOME)
4 Things that people must have to live are called ________. (NEEDS)
6 Things that are made or grown are called ________. (GOODS)
7 The amount of money you pay to buy something is its ________. (PRICE)
8 A bank service that lets people keep their money safe is a ________. (SAVINGS ACCOUNT)

DOWN
1 Things that people would like to have are called ________. (WANTS)
3 A place to buy and sell things is a ________. (MARKET)
5 Jobs people do to help others are called ________. (SERVICES)

Tell someone in your family what you have learned about work and money.

©Curriculum Associates, Inc. *Passwords: Social Studies Vocabulary, Book B, Lesson 7* 79

LESSON 8 Producing Goods

(Student Book pages 46–51)

Lesson Summary Consumers buy goods. Producers make or grow goods. Some producers sell goods that they grow. Others sell goods that are made in a factory. Trade is the buying and selling of goods and services. Consumers can use money to buy goods, or they can barter for them. Factories specialize and use technology to produce goods.

TARGET VOCABULARY

producers people who make or grow goods to sell

consumers people who buy goods

trade the buying and selling of goods and services

barter trading goods or services without using money

factory a place where goods are made

scarcity when there are not enough goods to meet people's needs

specialize choosing to grow or make just one product

technology the use of science to make new things

COGNATES

Spanish-speaking students may find a discussion of the similarities and differences between English and Spanish cognates helpful.

English	Spanish
producers	productores
consumers	consumidores
scarcity	escasez
specialize	especializarse
technology	tecnología

BEFORE READING

Activate Prior Knowledge  

Ask a volunteer to give the meaning of goods (*things that are made or grown*). Show students pictures of a variety of goods in advertising flyers from supermarkets and department stores. Point to food items and ask students to talk about where the foods come from. Then point to items such as clothing and housewares. Ask students where they think these things are made.

Introduce Target Vocabulary  

Tell students they are about to read a selection about how goods are produced. Write the target vocabulary words on the board. Model the pronunciation of each word and have student volunteers repeat the word. Discuss the meaning of each word and, if necessary, write the definition next to the word.

Present Graphic Organizer 

Provide each student with a copy of Vocabulary Graphic Organizer: Four Square, Teacher Guide page 67. Have students choose or assign each student a target vocabulary word. Tell students to write their word in the center square. As they read, students should add information about the target word to the graphic organizer.

Word and Definition Cards for Lesson 8 are on pages 99 and 100 of the Teacher Guide.

VOCABULARY STRATEGY: Use Illustrations

Illustrations can provide reinforcement for the words and concepts introduced in the lesson. Tell students to look at the first illustration on page 46. Point to Meg and remind students that she is a farmer. Ask *Is Meg a consumer or a producer in this picture?* (a producer) *What goods does she produce?* (apples) Ask similar questions about the other illustrations in the lesson, using as many target vocabulary words as possible. Remind students to refer to illustrations, here and in other lessons, to get a better idea of unknown words.

LESSON 8

producers consumers trade barter factory scarcity specialize technology

We all need or want to buy goods. Where do the goods come from? Keep reading to find out.

Producing Goods

Producers make or grow goods to sell. Meg grows apples. She is a producer. She sells her goods at a store. People come to the store to buy the apples. People who buy goods are **consumers**. They eat or use the things a producer makes.

A consumer buys the apples that Meg grows.

Trading Goods

Trade is the buying and selling of goods and services. When Meg sells her apples, she takes money. That is a trade. Sometimes people trade goods but do not use money. This is called **barter**. Meg gives Lee apples. Lee gives Meg honey. Trading honey for apples is barter.

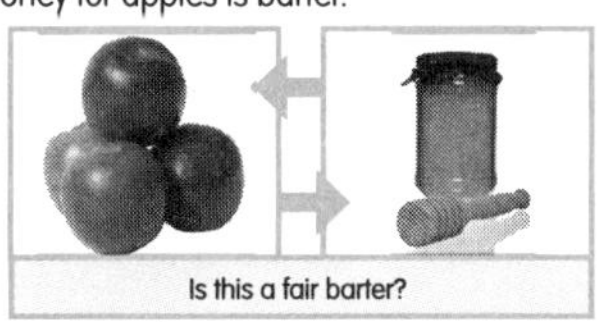
Is this a fair barter?

46 Producing Goods

How People Make Goods

Alex is a producer. He has a **factory**. It is a place where goods are made. Alex knows that there is a scarcity of shoes. A **scarcity** happens when there is not enough of something. People need more shoes. Alex decides to make some. His factory will **specialize**. It will make just one thing. Alex will be able to sell many shoes.

What kind of shoes are made at this factory?

New Ways to Make Goods

Alex uses technology to make shoes. **Technology** uses science to make new things. Alex has machines at his factory. A machine is a kind of technology. It helps Alex make more shoes.

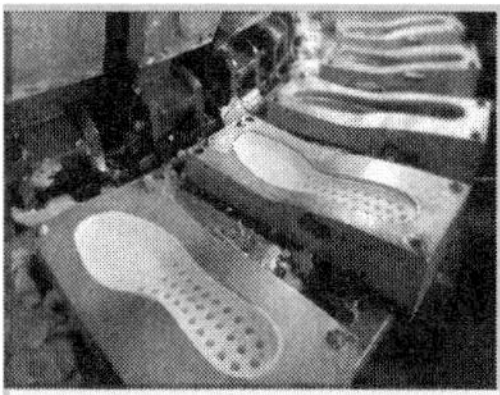
Technology helps to make more shoes each day.

My Social Studies Words

Go to page 79 to list the other words you have learned about producing goods.

Producing Goods 47

DURING READING 

Read the selection aloud to students as they follow along in their books, pausing at the end of each paragraph or section. Review any words or concepts that students are having trouble with. Remind students that there is a glossary at the back of the student book that contains all of the words that appear in boldfaced type in the lesson.

- Direct students' attention to the words *producers* and *consumers*. Ask them how the words are similar. (*They both end with* -ers.) Remind students that the suffix *-er* means "someone who," as in *teacher* and *leader*. Explain that a producer produces, or creates, something. A consumer consumes, or uses, something.
- Use the illustration at the bottom of page 46 to review the concept of bartering. Ask students what Meg's neighbor bartered for the apples (*a jar of honey*). Ask students if they think the barter was fair. Are the items being bartered of equal, or nearly equal, value?
- Have students look at the photographs on page 47. Ask students to tell about the pictures, using the target vocabulary words *producer, factory, specialize,* and *technology*.
- Write the word *technology* on the board. Circle each syllable. Guide students to pronounce the word as they clap out the syllables. Then have students say the word and use it in a sentence.

Have students read the passage again on their own.

AFTER READING

Review Graphic Organizer  

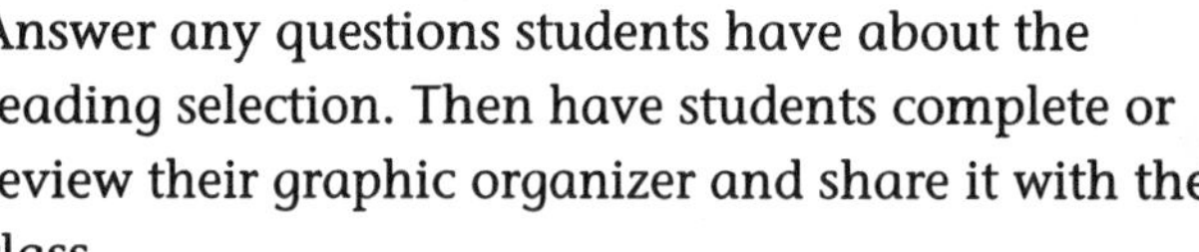

Answer any questions students have about the reading selection. Then have students complete or review their graphic organizer and share it with the class.

My Social Studies Words 

Encourage students to turn to My Social Studies Words on page 79 of the student book and use the space provided to add other words about producing goods.

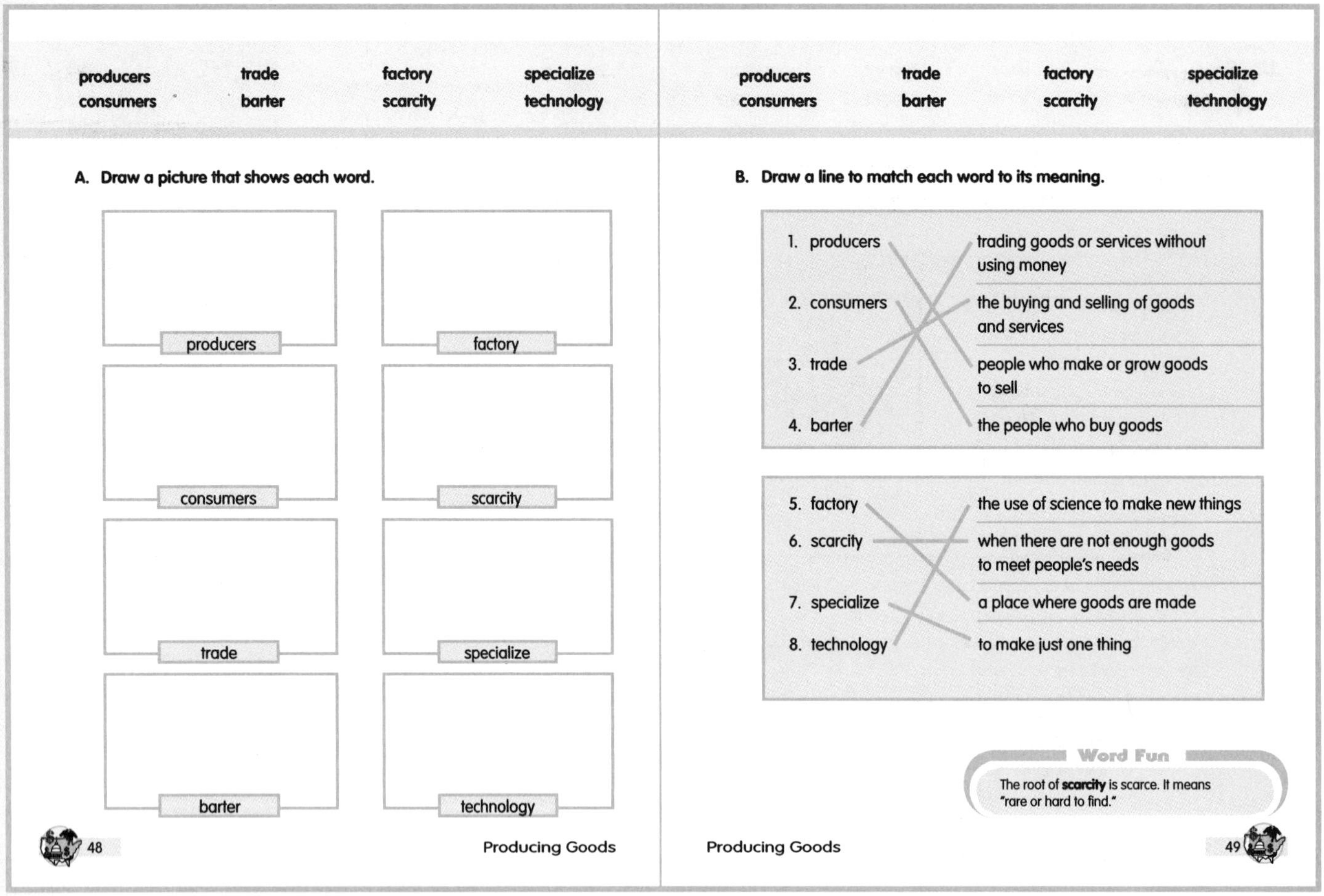

producers	trade	factory	specialize
consumers	barter	scarcity	technology

A. Draw a picture that shows each word.

producers	factory
consumers	scarcity
trade	specialize
barter	technology

producers	trade	factory	specialize
consumers	barter	scarcity	technology

B. Draw a line to match each word to its meaning.

1. producers	trading goods or services without using money
2. consumers	the buying and selling of goods and services
3. trade	people who make or grow goods to sell
4. barter	the people who buy goods

5. factory	the use of science to make new things
6. scarcity	when there are not enough goods to meet people's needs
7. specialize	a place where goods are made
8. technology	to make just one thing

Word Fun

The root of **scarcity** is scarce. It means "rare or hard to find."

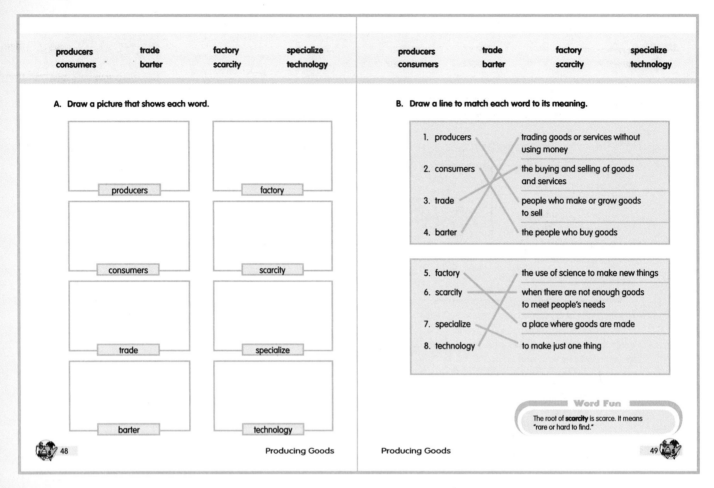

ACTIVITIES A–C

Encourage students to complete as many of the activities as possible. Remind students that they may refer to the Glossary at the back of their book as they complete the activities. Students may work independently, in small groups, or as a class. When students are done, discuss the answers for each activity.

Extensions 

These extension ideas allow you to reuse or expand upon the activities. Share them with students who complete the activities before other students, or have students do them for additional practice with target vocabulary words.

A Write the vocabulary words in alphabetical order.

B Find and write the five vocabulary words that have three or more syllables. Draw lines between the syllables in each word. Compare your words with a partner's.

C Choose one of the sentences you completed on page 50. Draw a picture to illustrate the sentence.

WORD FUN

Remind students that the word *scarce* means "rare or hard to find." Have students draw a picture of something they think is scarce. Display the pictures so students can compare their ideas.

producers	trade	factory	specialize
consumers	barter	scarcity	technology

C. Use a word from above to finish each sentence.

1. This new ___technology___ will make shoes faster and cheaper.
2. We went to the truck ___factory___ to see how trucks are made.
3. The people who make toys are ___producers___ .
4. The people buying food in a market are ___consumers___ .
5. Let's ___barter___ . I'll give you my milk. You give me your apple.
6. This class has a ___scarcity___ of pencils. We have almost none left.
7. These bakers ___specialize___ in making bread.
8. In a store, ___trade___ happens all day long.

50 Producing Goods

producers	trade	factory	specialize
consumers	barter	scarcity	technology

Write!

Tell about a time when you bartered with a friend. What did you give your friend? What did your friend give you? Was the barter a good way to get what you wanted?

Answers will vary. See sample answer.

Producing Goods 51

Write!

Provide each student with a copy of Writing Graphic Organizer: Web on Teacher Guide page 71, to use before they start writing. Students should write "When I Bartered" in the center circle. In the surrounding circles, they should write words and phrases that tell who they bartered with, what items were traded, and how they felt about the experience.

Sample Answer

I bartered when I traded a book for my friend's toy car. It was a good trade because I had already read the book and I wanted a toy car. My friend had other cars and he wanted to read my book. We were both happy with the trade.

TAKE-HOME ACTIVITY

Assign the Take-Home Activity to students for additional practice with the target vocabulary words. The reproducible Take-Home Activity for Lesson 8 is on page 80 of the Teacher Guide.

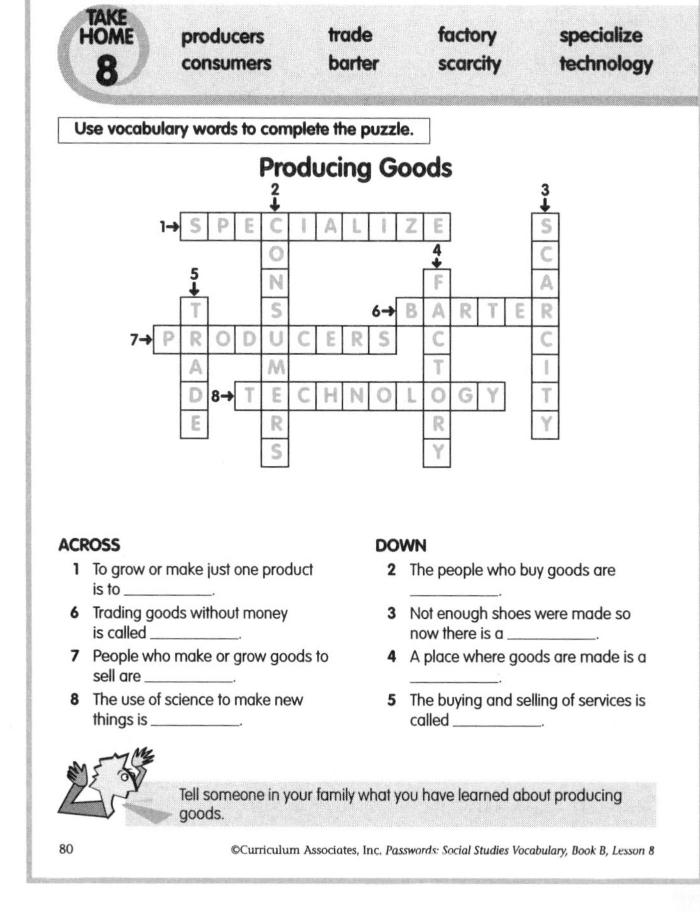

TAKE HOME 8

producers	trade	factory	specialize
consumers	barter	scarcity	technology

Use vocabulary words to complete the puzzle.

Producing Goods

ACROSS

1 To grow or make just one product is to ________.
6 Trading goods without money is called ________.
7 People who make or grow goods to sell are ________.
8 The use of science to make new things is ________.

DOWN

2 The people who buy goods are ________.
3 Not enough shoes were made so now there is a ________.
4 A place where goods are made is a ________.
5 The buying and selling of services is called ________.

Tell someone in your family what you have learned about producing goods.

80

Communities Change

(Student Book pages 52–57)

Lesson Summary Pioneers are the first group of people to live in a place. Pioneers live in the wilderness without many people around. A group of pioneers can change an area of wilderness into a settlement by building homes and growing food. If settlements are centers for transportation and communication, they may become cities.

TARGET VOCABULARY

history what we know about the past

wilderness a natural place without towns or people around

pioneer the first person to live in a place

settlement a small, new town

transportation a way of moving things or people from one place to another

steamboat a boat that gets power from boiling water

communication sharing information

skyscraper a very tall building

COGNATES

Spanish-speaking students may find a discussion of the similarities and differences between English and Spanish cognates helpful.

English	Spanish
history	historía
pioneer	pionero
transportation	transporte
communication	comunicación

BEFORE READING

Activate Prior Knowledge  

Tell students that a *community* is a place where people live. Write the title of the lesson in the center of a concept web. Ask students to suggest ways that communities change over many years. If necessary, prompt their thinking by asking questions about components of your own community, such as roads, stores, and parks. Record their ideas in the web.

Introduce Target Vocabulary  

Tell students they are about to read a selection about how communities change. Write the target vocabulary words on the board. Model the pronunciation of each word and have student volunteers repeat the word. Discuss the meaning of each word and, if necessary, write the definition next to the word.

Present Graphic Organizer 

Provide each student with a copy of Vocabulary Graphic Organizer: Word Web, Teacher Guide page 68. Assign each student a target vocabulary word. Have students write the word in the center circle of the web. As students read, they should add information about the target vocabulary word in the remaining circles. Depending on the word, students might illustrate their word and write a definition of the word, a sentence using the word, and the plural form of the word.

Word and Definition Cards for Lesson 9 are on pages 101 and 102 of the Teacher Guide.

VOCABULARY STRATEGY: Compound Words

Tell students that a compound word is a word made by combining two smaller words. Tell them that two of the target vocabulary words are compound words and ask them to identify them (*steamboat, skyscraper*). Then ask them to tell what smaller words were used to make each compound word. Explain how visualizing the two smaller words in a compound word can help them remember its meaning.

LESSON 9

history	pioneer	transportation	communication
wilderness	settlement	steamboat	skyscraper

Are there old buildings in your community? Are new buildings going up? How does a community change? Keep reading to find out.

Communities Change

History is what we know about the past. Jean du Sable is part of Chicago's history.

Jean du Sable, a pioneer, was born in 1745.

Long ago, Chicago was a large, natural place. No one lived there. This kind of place is called a **wilderness**. Jean du Sable was the first person to live there. He was a **pioneer**.

A Settlement Begins

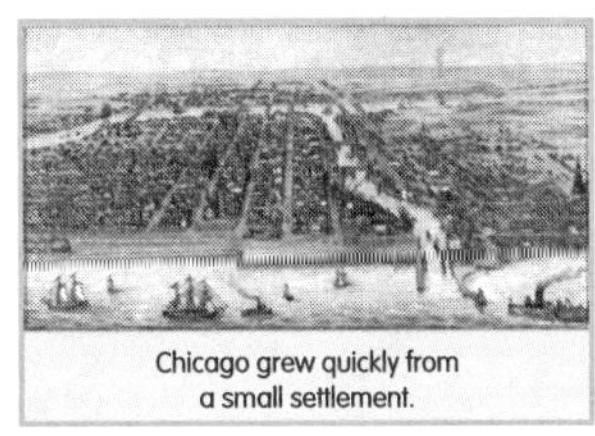
Chicago grew quickly from a small settlement.

Jean du Sable built a house. He kept cows and sheep. He planted a garden. He then told new people about his place. Some of them built homes near his. Soon there was a **settlement**. It was a small, new town.

52 Communities Change

Towns Need Transportation

This steamboat carried people and goods.

The town was on a river. The river flowed into a lake. The river and lake were good for **transportation**. This is a way of moving people or goods from place to place. People first came to the town in small boats. Later, they came in steamboats. A **steamboat** gets its power from boiling water.

Sharing Information in Towns

People came to the town for trade. The town was a good place for **communication**. That is how people share news and ideas.

Chicago Today

Millions of people work or live in Chicago's skyscrapers.

Today, Chicago is a huge city. It has skyscrapers. A **skyscraper** is a very tall building. The wild place has changed to a busy city.

My Social Studies Words

Go to page 80 to list the other words you have learned about how communities change.

Communities Change 53

DURING READING 

Read the selection aloud to students as they follow along in their books, pausing at the end of each paragraph or section. Review any words or concepts that students are having trouble with. Remind students that there is a glossary at the back of the student book that contains all of the words that appear in boldfaced type in the lesson.

- Give students information about Jean du Sable (zhahn doo sah-bluh) as they look at the illustration of him on page 52. Tell them that his father was from France and his mother was from Haiti. He set up a trading post and traded fur and grain with the Native Americans in the area. The buildings in his trading post were the first permanent buildings in the wilderness where he lived.
- Discuss the picture of the early settlement on page 52 and the picture of modern-day Chicago on page 53. Create a Venn diagram on the board to record students' ideas about how the places are similar and different.
- Point out the word *transportation* and remind students that transportation is "a way of moving things or people from one place to another." Discuss the modes of transportation that were available when the Chicago area was a settlement (*horses, boats, wagons*) and the ones available there today (*cars, planes, trains*).
- Make sure that students understand what *steam* is. If necessary, explain that steam is the hot, wet air that rises above boiling water. Ask students to raise their hands if they have ever seen steam. Then explain that large amounts of steam can make engines work.

Have students read the passage again on their own.

AFTER READING

Review Graphic Organizer 

Answer any questions students have about the reading selection. Then have students complete or review their graphic organizer and share it with the class.

My Social Studies Words 

Encourage students to turn to My Social Studies Words on page 80 of the student book and use the space provided to add other words about how communities change.

history | pioneer | transportation | communication
wilderness | settlement | steamboat | skyscraper

A. Circle the word that goes with each picture.

1.  steamboat / wilderness / (skyscraper)
2.  settlement / (pioneer) / skyscraper
3.  (settlement) / wilderness / transportation
4.  pioneer / (steamboat) / communication
5.  (history) / skyscraper / steamboat
6.  settlement / history / (communication)
7.  (wilderness) / settlement / pioneer
8.  history / wilderness / (transportation)

54 Communities Change

history | pioneer | transportation | communication
wilderness | settlement | steamboat | skyscraper

B. Fill in the blanks with the correct word from above.

1. a way of sharing news and ideas c o m m u n i c a t i o n
2. what we know about the past h i s t o r y
3. one of the first people to live in a place p i o n e e r
4. a large natural place where no one lives w i l d e r n e s s
5. a very tall building s k y s c r a p e r
6. a way of moving people or goods from place to place t r a n s p o r t a t i o n
7. a boat that gets its power from boiling water s t e a m b o a t
8. a small, new town s e t t l e m e n t

Word Fun

A **skyscraper** is so tall that it seems to scrape, or touch, the sky.

Communities Change 55

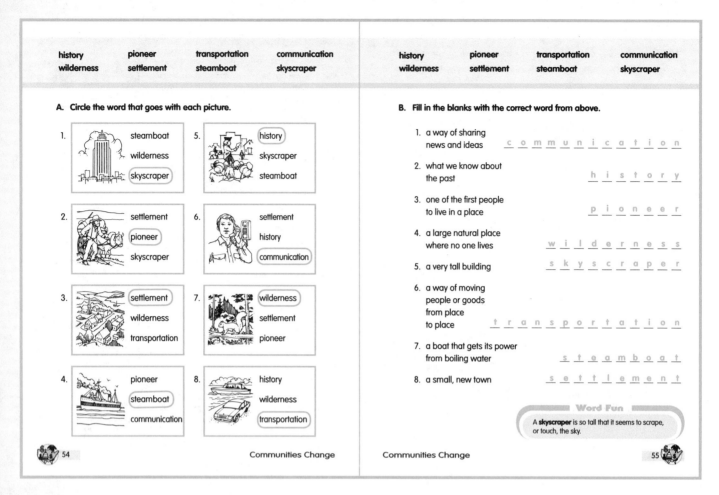

ACTIVITIES A–C

Encourage students to complete as many of the activities as possible. Remind students that they may refer to the Glossary at the back of their book as they complete the activities. Students may work independently, in small groups, or as a class. When students are done, discuss the answers for each activity.

Extensions 

These extension ideas allow you to reuse or expand upon the activities. Share them with students who complete the activities before other students, or have students do them for additional practice with target vocabulary words.

A Choose a target vocabulary word. Make as many words as possible using only the letters found in that word.

B Write the numbers 2, 3, 4, and 5 at the top of a sheet of paper. Under each number, write the target vocabulary words that have that many syllables.

C Choose one of the sentences you completed on page 56. Draw a picture to go with it.

WORD FUN

Explain to students that there is no height requirement that makes a tall building a *skyscraper*. Tell them that many people say that buildings have to be at least 100 stories, or floors, tall to be called a *skyscraper*.

history	**pioneer**	**transportation**	**communication**
wilderness	**settlement**	**steamboat**	**skyscraper**

C. Use a word from above to finish each sentence.

1. They are building the world's tallest ___skyscraper___ in that city.
2. If you study ___history___, you will learn about the past.
3. In this area, the earliest ___settlement___ was a few houses built along the river.
4. Boiling water gives a ___steamboat___ its power.
5. The phone is one tool for ___communication___.
6. A bike is a kind of ___transportation___.
7. Jean du Sable was the first ___pioneer___ in the area that is now Chicago.
8. You might find a bear deep in the ___wilderness___.

56 Communities Change

history	**pioneer**	**transportation**	**communication**
wilderness	**settlement**	**steamboat**	**skyscraper**

Write!

What was your community like long ago? How did people get from one place to another? Was communication easy? Why or why not?

Answers will vary. See sample answer.

Communities Change 57

Write! 

Provide each student with a copy of Writing Graphic Organizer: Details Cube on Teacher Guide page 72, to use before they start writing. Tell students to read the question carefully, then think about the details they will include in their answers. Tell students to write words or phrases in the boxes of the cube. Explain that these words and phrases are the details they will include in their answers.

Sample Answer

Long ago, my community was wilderness. The pioneers came. They built a settlement. They used horses for transportation. I think communication was hard. There were no telephones or computers then.

TAKE-HOME ACTIVITY 

Assign the Take-Home Activity to students for additional practice with the target vocabulary words. The reproducible Take-Home Activity for Lesson 9 is on page 81 of the Teacher Guide.

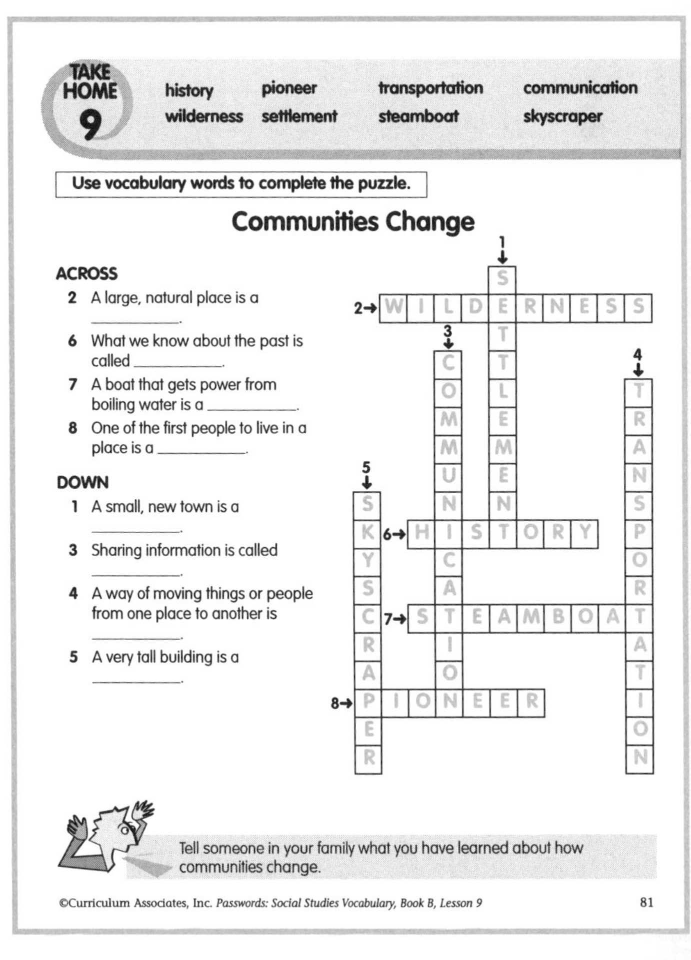

TAKE HOME 9

history	**pioneer**	**transportation**	**communication**
wilderness	**settlement**	**steamboat**	**skyscraper**

Use vocabulary words to complete the puzzle.

Communities Change

ACROSS

2 A large, natural place is a ________.

6 What we know about the past is called ________.

7 A boat that gets power from boiling water is a ________.

8 One of the first people to live in a place is a ________.

DOWN

1 A small, new town is a ________.

3 Sharing information is called ________.

4 A way of moving things or people from one place to another is ________.

5 A very tall building is a ________.

Tell someone in your family what you have learned about how communities change.

 81

LESSON 10 Communities Near and Far

(Student Book pages 58–63)

Lesson Summary A culture is a way of life for a group of people. The people in a culture share their beliefs. Customs and traditions are things that people in a culture do at a certain time, in the same way, year after year. When people in a culture celebrate, they honor a special day by doing something special. For example, they might celebrate by having a ceremony. People in a culture also share legends, stories about things that happened long ago. Storytellers are the people who tell these stories.

TARGET VOCABULARY

culture a way of life for a group of people

belief something we think is true

custom something that people usually do at a certain time

celebrate to honor a special day

tradition something that people do the same way year after year

ceremony an event with special words and actions

legend a story about things that happened long ago

storyteller a person who tells stories

COGNATES

Spanish-speaking students may find a discussion of the similarities and differences between English and Spanish cognates helpful.

English	Spanish
culture	cultura
custom	costumbre
celebrate	celebrar
tradition	tradición
ceremony	ceremonia
legend	leyenda

BEFORE READING

Activate Prior Knowledge

Have students follow along as you read the introductory paragraph above the title. Ask students to name special days when they give or receive gifts, such as birthdays, anniversaries, or holidays. Encourage them to talk about the foods they eat on these special days. Then have students share their ideas about why people celebrate or observe special days with gifts and special foods.

Introduce Target Vocabulary

Tell students they are about to read a selection about how different cultures celebrate special days. Write the target vocabulary words on the board. Model the pronunciation of each word and have student volunteers repeat the word. Discuss the meaning of each word and, if necessary, write the definition next to the word.

Present Graphic Organizer

Provide each student with a copy of Vocabulary Graphic Organizer: Knowledge Scale, Teacher Guide page 69. Have students list the target vocabulary words in the first column. Then tell students to make a check mark for each word in the appropriate column. As they read, students should add definitions for the target vocabulary words in the last column.

Word and Definition Cards for Lesson 10 are on pages 103 and 104 of the Teacher Guide.

VOCABULARY STRATEGY: Print Features

Remind students why a word might appear in boldfaced, or darker, type in a textbook. (*It is an important word. It is a new word.*) Tell students that they can often find the meaning of a boldfaced word close to where the word appears in the text. Refer students to the first paragraph of the lesson.

Ask what words are in darker type than the other words (*culture, belief*). Then guide students to find the meanings of *culture* and *belief* in the paragraph. As they read the lesson, have students draw an arrow from each boldfaced word to the sentence that gives the word's meaning.

LESSON 10

culture, belief, custom, celebrate, tradition, ceremony, legend, storyteller

On some special days, we give gifts. Sometimes we eat special food. Why do we do that? Read to find out.

Communities Near and Far

Culture is a way of life for a group of people. The group shares beliefs. A **belief** is something we think is true. Asha lives in India. Some people there believe they should not eat beef.

Eating beef is not part of Asha's culture.

People Have Different Customs

A **custom** is something people do at a certain time. Eating cake is a custom for a birthday. It is one way to celebrate the day. When we **celebrate**, we do something special. Each culture has its own birthday customs.

Mexican children celebrate a birthday with a piñata.

58 Communities Near and Far

People Follow Traditions

A **tradition** is something that people do the same way each year. Ling lives in China. Each New Year, people there have a parade.

A **ceremony** is an event with special words and actions. A wedding is a ceremony. In one culture, the groom breaks a glass with his foot. That ends the wedding.

Why is the glass wrapped in a cloth for this wedding ceremony?

Stories Tell About Culture

A **legend** is a made-up story. Legends have been passed on for many years. In the past, no one wrote down the stories. A **storyteller** told them.

Do you know the legend of Paul Bunyan? He was a giant with a big blue ox. Paul Bunyan was very strong. He could cut down a tree with one blow.

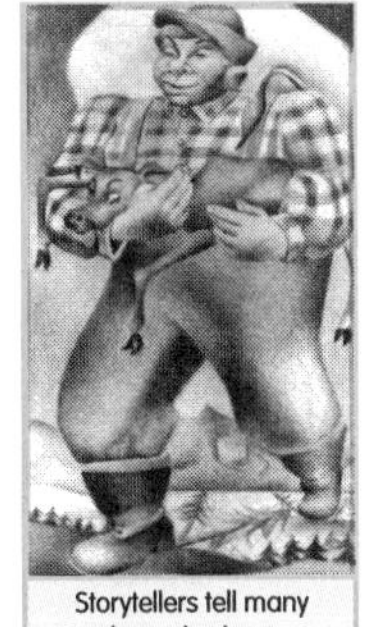

Storytellers tell many legends about Paul Bunyan.

My Social Studies Words

Go to page 80 to list the other words you have learned about communities near and far.

Communities Near and Far 59

DURING READING 

Read the selection aloud to students as they follow along in their books, pausing at the end of each paragraph or section. Review any words or concepts that students are having trouble with. Remind students that there is a glossary at the back of the student book that contains all of the words that appear in boldfaced type in the lesson.

- Read aloud the sentence "A belief is something we think is true" on page 58. Write the word *believe* on the board. Explain that *believe* means "to accept that something is true." Tell students that *belief* and *believe* are in the same word family. Discuss other words in the word family (*beliefs, believes, believed, believer*).
- Write the words *celebrate* and *ceremony* on the board. Guide students to pronounce the words. Point out that the initial consonant *c* makes the sound of *s* in both words. Then, point out the illustration at the top of page 59 and ask students to identify the ceremony that celebrates the marriage of two people (*a wedding*).
- Point out that the word *storyteller* is a compound word made up of the two smaller words *story* and *teller*. Explain that the meaning of the word is based on the meanings of both words: a person who tells stories. Talk about storytellers children have heard at school, the library, or in the community.

Have students read the passage again on their own.

AFTER READING

Review Graphic Organizer 

Answer any questions students have about the reading selection. Then have students complete or review their graphic organizer and share it with the class.

My Social Studies Words 

Encourage students to turn to My Social Studies Words on page 80 of the student book and use the space provided to add other words about communities near and far.

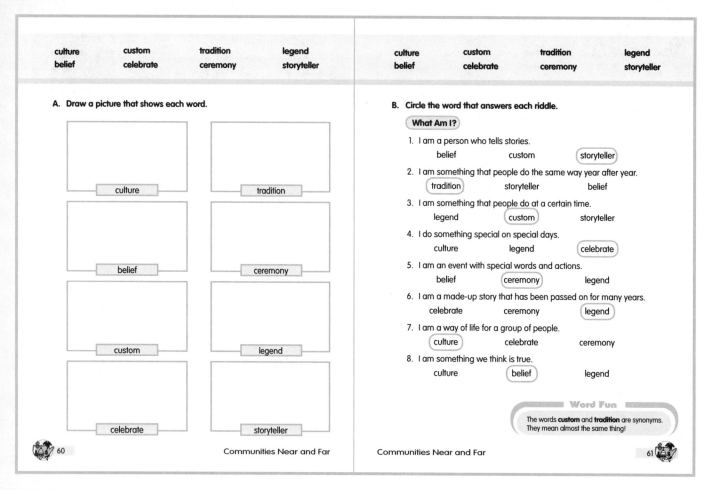

culture custom tradition legend
belief celebrate ceremony storyteller

A. Draw a picture that shows each word.

culture | tradition
belief | ceremony
custom | legend
celebrate | storyteller

60 Communities Near and Far

culture custom tradition legend
belief celebrate ceremony storyteller

B. Circle the word that answers each riddle.

What Am I?

1. I am a person who tells stories.
belief custom **storyteller**
2. I am something that people do the same way year after year.
tradition storyteller belief
3. I am something that people do at a certain time.
legend **custom** storyteller
4. I do something special on special days.
culture legend **celebrate**
5. I am an event with special words and actions.
belief **ceremony** legend
6. I am a made-up story that has been passed on for many years.
celebrate ceremony **legend**
7. I am a way of life for a group of people.
culture celebrate ceremony
8. I am something we think is true.
culture **belief** legend

Word Fun

The words **custom** and **tradition** are synonyms. They mean almost the same thing!

Communities Near and Far 61

ACTIVITIES A–C

Encourage students to complete as many of the activities as possible. Remind students that they may refer to the Glossary at the back of their book as they complete the activities. Students may work independently, in small groups, or as a class. When students are done, discuss the answers for each activity.

Extensions 

These extension ideas allow you to reuse or expand upon the activities. Share them with students who complete the activities before other students, or have students do them for additional practice with target vocabulary words.

A Write the target vocabulary word that would come before the others in the list in a dictionary (*belief*). Then write the target vocabulary word that would come after all the others (*tradition*).

B Write the numbers 2, 3, and 4 across the top of a sheet of paper. Under each number, write the target vocabulary words that have that many syllables.

C With a partner, choose one target vocabulary word. Write a sentence using that word. Then compare your sentence with your partner's sentence.

WORD FUN

Write the words *custom* and *tradition* on the board. Pronounce the words and then have students pronounce them with you. Review that a *custom* is something that people usually do at a certain time. Talk about a custom in your classroom, such as a way to celebrate finishing a book. Ask students to tell about customs from their classrooms in the past. Then review that a *tradition* is something that people do the same way year after year. Talk about a tradition in your school, such as the observance of a holiday, a school fair, or a field day event.

culture	custom	tradition	legend
belief	celebrate	ceremony	storyteller

C. Use a word from above to finish each sentence.

1. On birthdays, it is a ___custom___ to have cake.
2. A wedding is a special kind of ___ceremony___ .
3. When we ___celebrate___ Thanksgiving, we eat turkey.
4. Have you ever heard the ___legend___ about how the rabbit lost its tail?
5. The children go to the library to listen to a ___storyteller___ .
6. It is my ___belief___ that we should be good to the earth.
7. China has a long ___tradition___ of celebrating the new year with a parade.
8. People live in grass houses in one ___culture___ .

62 Communities Near and Far

culture	custom	tradition	legend
belief	celebrate	ceremony	storyteller

Write!

What traditions do you have? How does your family celebrate special days? Tell about the traditions in your home.

Answers will vary. See sample answer.

Communities Near and Far 63

Write! 

Have students work with a partner to brainstorm ideas for writing. Then provide each student with a copy of Writing Graphic Organizer: Web, Teacher Guide page 71, to use before they start writing. In the center circle, students should identify a special tradition. In the other circles, they should write ideas that describe the tradition. Provide students with a sentence starter such as, *At my house we have a birthday tradition.* Guide them to incorporate their ideas into sentences.

Sample Answer

At my house we have a birthday tradition. On your birthday, you get to choose the food for dinner. You don't have to do any chores. You get any kind of cake that you want.

TAKE-HOME ACTIVITY

Assign the Take-Home Activity to students for additional practice with the target vocabulary words. The reproducible Take-Home Activity for Lesson 10 is on page 82 of the Teacher Guide.

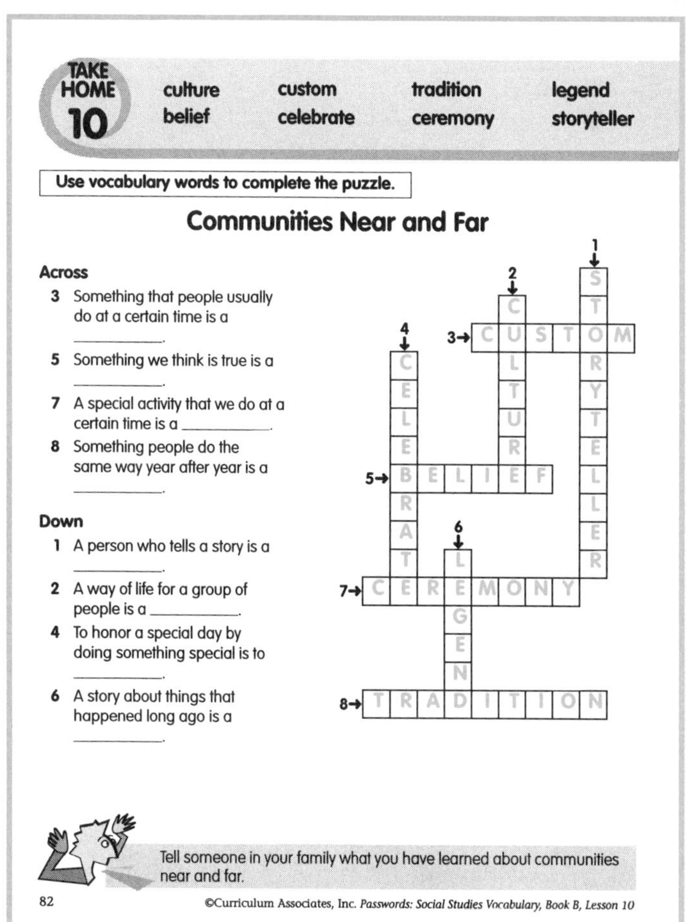

TAKE HOME 10

culture	custom	tradition	legend
belief	celebrate	ceremony	storyteller

Use vocabulary words to complete the puzzle.

Communities Near and Far

Across

3 Something that people usually do at a certain time is a ______. (CUSTOM)

5 Something we think is true is a ______. (BELIEF)

7 A special activity that we do at a certain time is a ______. (CEREMONY)

8 Something people do the same way year after year is a ______. (TRADITION)

Down

1 A person who tells a story is a ______. (STORYTELLER)

2 A way of life for a group of people is a ______. (CULTURE)

4 To honor a special day by doing something special is to ______. (CELEBRATE)

6 A story about things that happened long ago is a ______. (LEGEND)

Tell someone in your family what you have learned about communities near and far.

82 ©Curriculum Associates, Inc. *Passwords: Social Studies Vocabulary, Book B, Lesson 10*

Americans Come from Many Places

(Student Book pages 64–69)

Lesson Summary Countries have symbols, such as a flag. The Statue of Liberty is a symbol for freedom in America. Long ago, when immigrants came to America, their first stop was the Statue of Liberty. These immigrants made the long journey to America from many different lands. Although the journey was hard, the immigrants showed great courage.

TARGET VOCABULARY

symbol something that stands for something else

liberty another word for freedom

landmark something that helps people know a place

immigrant a person who moves from one country to another

ancestor a family member who lived before you

journey a long trip

courage what people show when they do something even though they are afraid

language the set of words people use to speak to each other

COGNATES

Spanish-speaking students may find a discussion of the similarities and differences between English and Spanish cognates helpful.

English	Spanish
symbol	símbolo
liberty	libertad
immigrant	inmigrante
language	lengua

BEFORE READING

Activate Prior Knowledge  

Talk about the different places students' families come from. Provide the sentence starter, "My family comes from <location>," and have students complete it. Display a world map, and mark the locations students name. Point out that people living in America have come from many different places. Save the map with markers for use in the During Reading activities.

Introduce Target Vocabulary  

Tell students they are about to read a selection about immigrants, people who came to America from other places. Write the target vocabulary words on the board. Model the pronunciation of each word and have student volunteers repeat the word. Discuss the meaning of each word and, if necessary, write the definition next to the word.

Present Graphic Organizer 

Provide each student with a copy of Vocabulary Graphic Organizer: Four Square, Teacher Guide page 67. Have students choose or assign each student a target vocabulary word. Tell students to write their word in the center square. As they read, students should add information about the target vocabulary word to the graphic organizer.

Word and Definition Cards for Lesson 11 are on pages 105 and 106 of the Teacher Guide.

VOCABULARY STRATEGY: Context Clues

Tell students that writers sometimes provide the meaning of a new word right before or right after the word is introduced. For example, in the sentence "A symbol stands for something else," the author directly provides the definition of *symbol*. Point out that the word "is" near the new word may signal a definition context clue. Ask students to circle the definition context clues they find in this lesson, draw an arrow to the word that each clue defines, and underline the word "is" in each sentence.

LESSON 11

symbol · landmark · ancestor · courage
liberty · immigrant · journey · language

Americans come from many countries. Can you name some other countries? Read to learn about people who come to live in the United States.

Americans Come from Many Places

A **symbol** stands for something else. Our flag is a symbol. It stands for our country.

The flag is a symbol of our country.

The Statue of Liberty

The Statue of Liberty is a symbol, too. It stands for **liberty**, or freedom. The statue is in New York. It is a landmark. A **landmark** is something that helps people know a place. Many saw the statue when they first came to our country.

The Statue of Liberty is a landmark.

A Land of Immigrants

A person who comes to live in a country is an **immigrant**. Our nation is a land of immigrants. Do you have ancestors who were not born here? An **ancestor** is a family member who lived before you.

Immigrants Come to America

Rose lives in America. Her ancestors came from Italy. They made the long trip. The **journey** was hard. But the immigrants showed great **courage**. They came here even though they were afraid.

Immigrants were happy to see the Statue of Liberty after their long journey across the ocean.

People came here from many lands. They spoke many languages. A **language** is the set of words people use to speak to one another. What language do you speak?

My Social Studies Words
Go to page 81 to list the other words you have learned about coming to America.

DURING READING

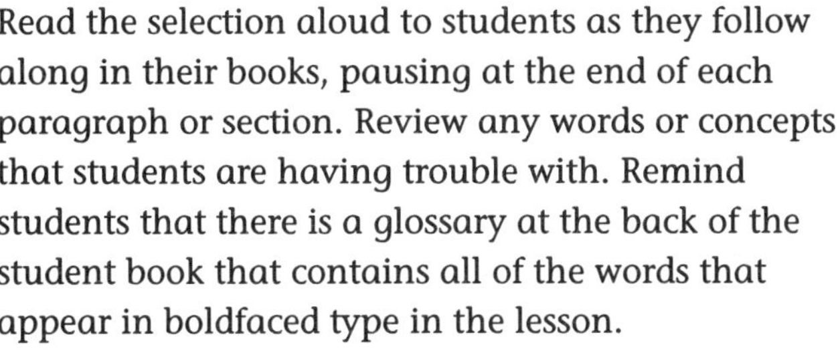

Read the selection aloud to students as they follow along in their books, pausing at the end of each paragraph or section. Review any words or concepts that students are having trouble with. Remind students that there is a glossary at the back of the student book that contains all of the words that appear in boldfaced type in the lesson.

- Review that a symbol is something that stands for something else. Write the symbols for addition and subtraction on the board. Point to the "plus" symbol, and explain that when we see this symbol, we know that we are supposed to add. Repeat for the "minus" symbol. Discuss other symbols students might recognize, such as on road signs.
- Talk about the different languages spoken in your school and in students' homes. Ask students whose families speak languages other than English at home to tell the name of the language they speak. Refer to the world map and connect the specific countries marked with the languages spoken in each.
- Remind students that the word *journey* is a noun meaning "a long trip." Explain that a journey might take a day or several days. Then tell students that the word *journey* can also be used as a verb meaning "to travel to a place." Model using *journey* in sentences, such as, "My family will take a journey to visit my grandparents." *(noun)* "We will journey for two days in the car." *(verb)* Provide opportunities for students to use the word *journey* in sentences, both as a noun and as a verb.

Have students read the passage again on their own.

AFTER READING

Review Graphic Organizer

Answer any questions students have about the reading selection. Then have students complete or review their graphic organizer and share it with the class.

My Social Studies Words

Encourage students to turn to My Social Studies Words on page 81 of the student book and use the space provided to add other words about immigrants who came to America.

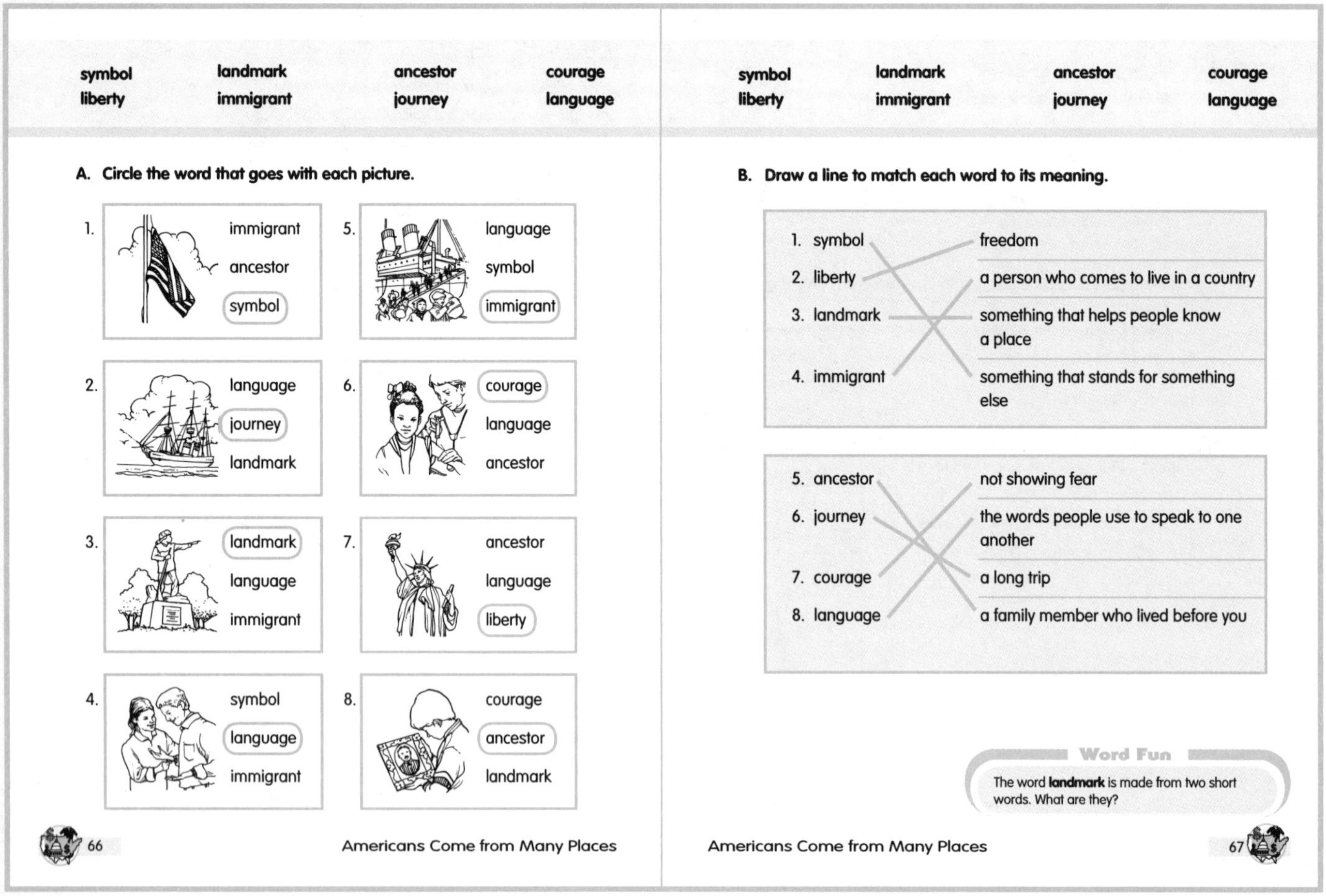

symbol	**landmark**	**ancestor**	**courage**
liberty	**immigrant**	**journey**	**language**

A. Circle the word that goes with each picture.

1. immigrant / ancestor / (symbol)
2. language / (journey) / landmark
3. (landmark) / language / immigrant
4. symbol / (language) / immigrant
5. language / symbol / (immigrant)
6. (courage) / language / ancestor
7. ancestor / language / (liberty)
8. courage / (ancestor) / landmark

66 Americans Come from Many Places

symbol	**landmark**	**ancestor**	**courage**
liberty	**immigrant**	**journey**	**language**

B. Draw a line to match each word to its meaning.

1. symbol	freedom
2. liberty	a person who comes to live in a country
3. landmark	something that helps people know a place
4. immigrant	something that stands for something else

5. ancestor	not showing fear
6. journey	the words people use to speak to one another
7. courage	a long trip
8. language	a family member who lived before you

Word Fun

The word **landmark** is made from two short words. What are they?

Americans Come from Many Places 67

ACTIVITIES A–C

Encourage students to complete as many of the activities as possible. Remind students that they may refer to the Glossary at the back of their book as they complete the activities. Students may work independently, in small groups, or as a class. When students are done, discuss the answers for each activity.

Extensions

These extension ideas allow you to reuse or expand upon the activities. Share them with students who complete the activities before other students, or have students do them for additional practice with target vocabulary words.

A List the target vocabulary words in alphabetical order. If you find two words that start with the same letter, write those words on the same line in your list.

B Make up a symbol that stands for the word *happy*. Share your symbol with a classmate and explain why you chose it.

C Some of the target words have smaller words in them. For example, the word *immigrant* contains the words *an* and *ant*. Write all the small words you can find in the word *landmark* (*land, mark, an, and*).

WORD FUN

Lead students to understand that *landmark* is a compound word made up of the two smaller words *land* and *mark*. Explain that the meaning of the word is based on the meanings of both words. Discuss landmarks near your school and near students' homes, as well as prominent ones in your city or community.

symbol, landmark, ancestor, courage, liberty, immigrant, journey, language

C. Use a word from above to finish each sentence.

1. What ___language___ do they speak in Italy?
2. That boy's ___ancestor___ lived in a log cabin long ago.
3. We let the bird go free. It was glad to get its ___liberty___.
4. A flag can be a ___symbol___ of a country.
5. The Statue of Liberty is a ___landmark___ in New York.
6. We drove all day to get here. It was a long ___journey___.
7. It takes ___courage___ to jump into the cold water.
8. Mr. Kung is an ___immigrant___ from China.

symbol, landmark, ancestor, courage, liberty, immigrant, journey, language

Write!

Tell about a time when you needed courage. What did you do?

Answers will vary. See sample answer.

Write! 

Have students work with a partner to brainstorm ideas for writing. Then provide each student with a copy of Writing Graphic Organizer: Details Cube, Teacher Guide page 72, to use before they start writing. Encourage students to think about a time when they needed courage. Tell them to write a detail about that time in each of the four squares. Then tell them to use their ideas to write their answers.

Sample Answer

I needed courage on my first day of school. I didn't know anyone. My teacher smiled at me. So I smiled at her. Then I smiled at everyone else. The other kids were nice to me. I was glad.

TAKE-HOME ACTIVITY

Assign the Take-Home Activity to students for additional practice with the target vocabulary words. The reproducible Take-Home Activity for Lesson 11 is on page 83 of the Teacher Guide.

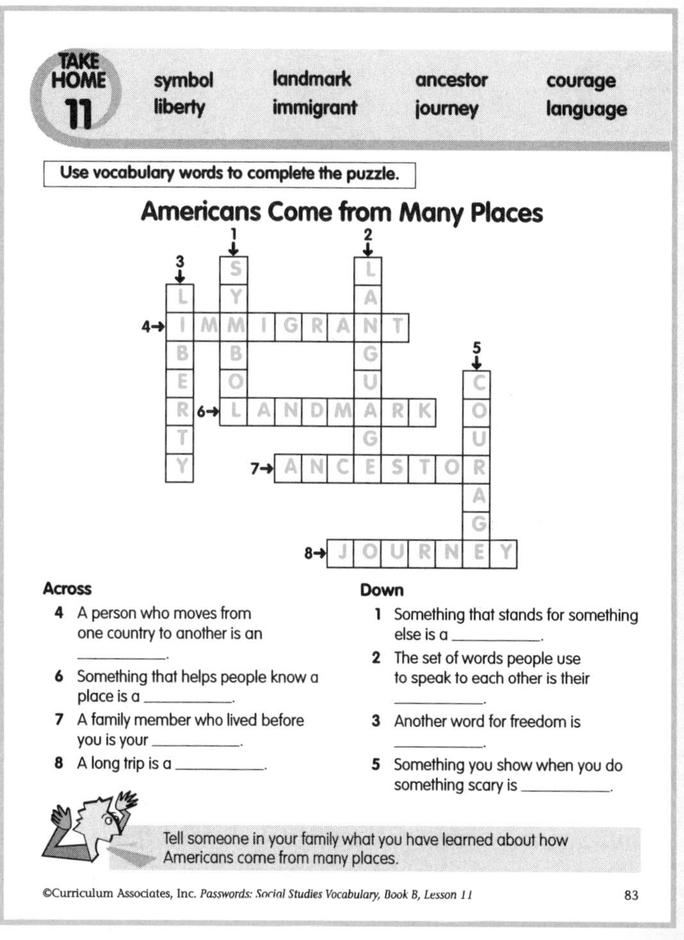

TAKE HOME 11

symbol, landmark, ancestor, courage, liberty, immigrant, journey, language

Use vocabulary words to complete the puzzle.

Americans Come from Many Places

Across

4 A person who moves from one country to another is an ________.

6 Something that helps people know a place is a ________.

7 A family member who lived before you is your ________.

8 A long trip is a ________.

Down

1 Something that stands for something else is a ________.

2 The set of words people use to speak to each other is their ________.

3 Another word for freedom is ________.

5 Something you show when you do something scary is ________.

Tell someone in your family what you have learned about how Americans come from many places.

 83

LESSON 12

Heroes and Holidays

(Student Book pages 70–75)

Lesson Summary National holidays are special days celebrated by everyone in a nation. Independence Day and Memorial Day are national holidays in the United States. On Memorial Day, Americans honor veterans, people who have fought in a war. Americans have also built monuments and memorials to honor these heroes. Religious holidays are special days for people of the same religion. Easter and Hanukkah are examples of religious holidays.

TARGET VOCABULARY

national holiday a special day for everyone in a nation

independence freedom from the rule of another country

memorial something that honors a person or event

honor to show we think highly of someone

hero a person who does brave or great things

monument a building or statue that honors a hero or event

veteran a person who fought in a war long ago

religious holiday a special day for people of the same religion

COGNATES

Spanish-speaking students may find a discussion of the similarities and differences between English and Spanish cognates helpful.

English	Spanish
independence	independencia
memorial	conmemorativo
honor	honor
hero	héroe
monument	monumento
veteran	veterano

BEFORE READING

Activate Prior Knowledge

Ask students to identify holidays they celebrate in school or with their families. List their responses on the board. Discuss the significance of each of the holidays listed. Then encourage students to describe how people celebrate each of these special days. Save the list of holidays on the board for use in the During Reading activities.

Introduce Target Vocabulary

Tell students they are about to read a selection about heroes and holidays. Write the target vocabulary words on the board. Model the pronunciation of each word and have student volunteers repeat the word. Discuss the meaning of each word and, if necessary, write the definition next to the word.

Present Graphic Organizer

Provide each student with a copy of Vocabulary Graphic Organizer: Four Square, Teacher Guide page 67. Have students choose or assign each student a target vocabulary word. Have students write the target vocabulary word in the middle space. As they read, students should add information about the word to their graphic organizers.

Word and Definition Cards for Lesson 12 are on pages 107 and 108 of the Teacher Guide.

VOCABULARY STRATEGY: Use Illustrations

Illustrations can provide reinforcement for the words and concepts students read about in the text. Guide students through a picture walk of the lesson before reading the text. Then, as you read, pause and ask students to describe what they see in the illustrations. Encourage them to use the target vocabulary words in their descriptions.

LESSON 12

national holiday **memorial** **hero** **veteran**
independence **honor** **monument** **religious holiday**

Your birthday is a special day. Nations also have special days. What might those days be? Read to find out.

Heroes and Holidays

Nations Have Holidays

A **national holiday** is a great day for the whole nation. Banks are closed. Most shops are closed. There is no mail. There is no school.

The Fourth of July is a national holiday. On this day, we celebrate our **independence**. That is freedom from the rule of another country.

Fireworks are popular on the Fourth of July when we celebrate our independence.

Holidays Show Respect

Memorial Day is a national holiday. A **memorial** makes us think about a person or an event from the past. We **honor** people who died in wars on this day. We show that we think highly of them. They were heroes. A **hero** does brave or great things.

The Lincoln Memorial honors Abraham Lincoln.

70 Heroes and Holidays

We Honor Our Heroes

We honor our heroes in many ways. Sometimes we build monuments. A **monument** is a building or statue. It honors a person or an event.

Lee is a hero. He fought in a war long ago. That makes him a **veteran**. There is a monument in Lee's town. It is in a park. It is for veterans of all wars.

This monument honors veterans.

Religions Have Holidays

We have religious holidays, too. A **religious holiday** is for people of the same religion. Easter is an example. Passover is too. Each day is a time to honor beliefs.

Passover is a special holiday for Jewish families.

My Social Studies Words

Go to page 81 to list other words you have learned about heroes and holidays.

Heroes and Holidays 71 

DURING READING 

Read the selection aloud to students as they follow along in their books, pausing at the end of each paragraph or section. Review any words or concepts that students are having trouble with. Remind students that there is a glossary at the back of the student book that contains all of the words that appear in boldfaced type in the lesson.

- Return to the list of holidays on the board. As you read the lesson, work with students to identify each holiday listed as a national holiday or a religious holiday. Encourage students to add other holidays to the list.
- Reinforce that a veteran is a person who fought in a war. Point out the monument in the illustration on page 71 and explain that monuments such as this one remind us of how brave the veterans were. Explain that on Memorial Day, people come out to honor the veterans who are marching, as well as those who have died.
- Work with students to create a concept web for the word *hero*. Write *hero* in the center circle in the web. As students identify heroes, add their names to the surrounding circles. Ask students to tell why each person named is considered a hero. Discuss types of heroes and characteristics of heroes.

Have students read the passage again on their own.

AFTER READING

Review Graphic Organizer 

Answer any questions students have about the reading selection. Then have students complete or review their graphic organizer and share it with the class.

My Social Studies Words 

Encourage students to turn to My Social Studies Words on page 81 of the student book and use the space provided to add other words about heroes and holidays.

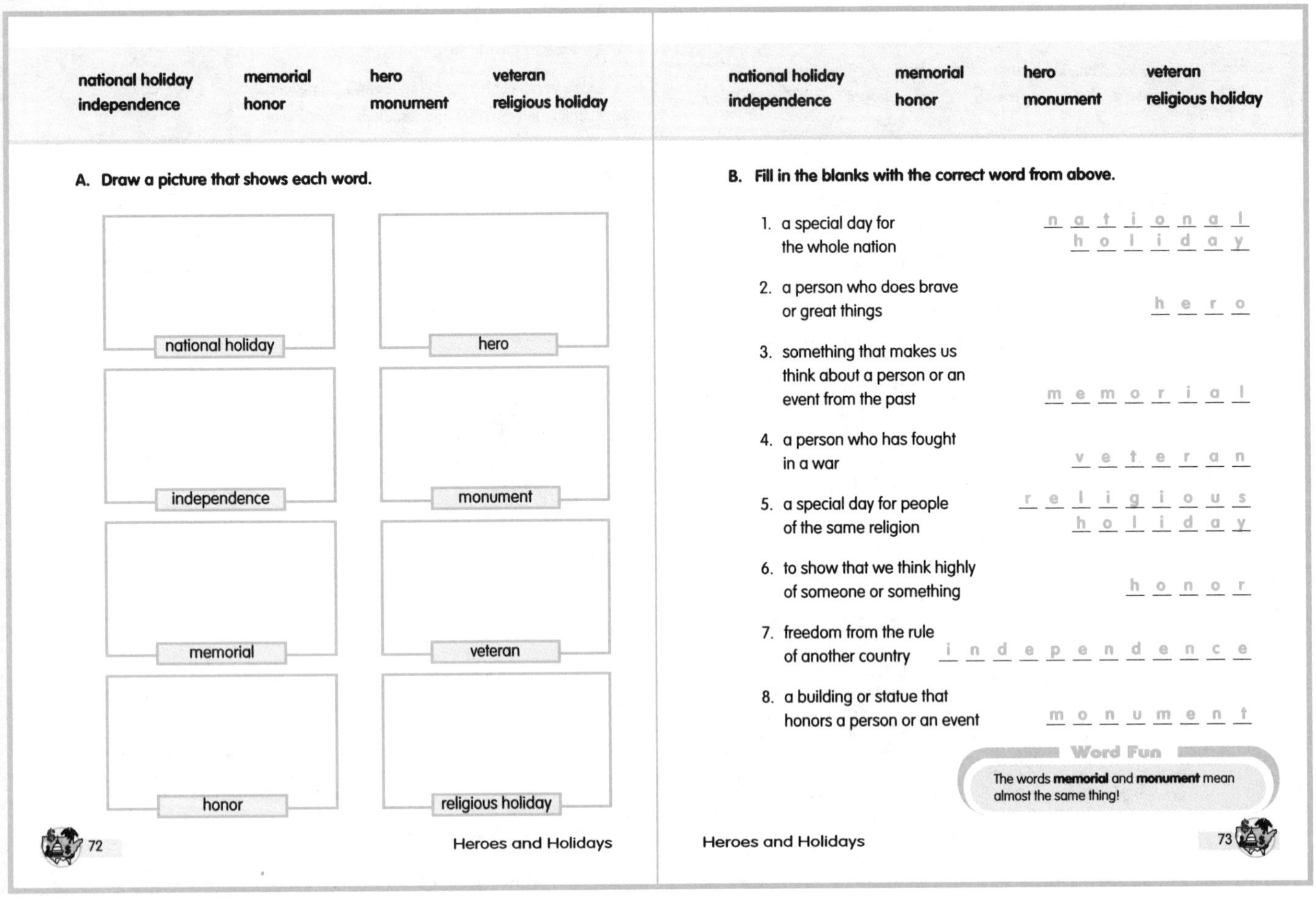

national holiday	memorial	hero	veteran
independence	honor	monument	religious holiday

A. Draw a picture that shows each word.

national holiday	hero
independence	monument
memorial	veteran
honor	religious holiday

national holiday	memorial	hero	veteran
independence	honor	monument	religious holiday

B. Fill in the blanks with the correct word from above.

1. a special day for the whole nation — n a t i o n a l h o l i d a y
2. a person who does brave or great things — h e r o
3. something that makes us think about a person or an event from the past — m e m o r i a l
4. a person who has fought in a war — v e t e r a n
5. a special day for people of the same religion — r e l i g i o u s h o l i d a y
6. to show that we think highly of someone or something — h o n o r
7. freedom from the rule of another country — i n d e p e n d e n c e
8. a building or statue that honors a person or an event — m o n u m e n t

Word Fun

The words **memorial** and **monument** mean almost the same thing!

ACTIVITIES A–C

Encourage students to complete as many of the activities as possible. Remind students that they may refer to the Glossary at the back of their book as they complete the activities. Students may work independently, in small groups, or as a class. When students are done, discuss the answers for each activity.

Extensions 

These extension ideas allow you to reuse or expand upon the activities. Share them with students who complete the activities before other students, or have students do them for additional practice with target vocabulary words.

A Circle the target vocabulary words with two syllables and underline the words with three syllables.

B Write a riddle for one of the target vocabulary words. Exchange riddles with a partner and solve each other's riddles.

C Draw a picture of your family celebrating a holiday. Write a sentence to label your picture. Use the word *holiday* in your sentence.

WORD FUN

Display photographs of the Lincoln Memorial and the Washington Monument. Explain to students that these structures were built to honor two American presidents. Tell students that the Washington Monument was built to honor George Washington, the first president. Then identify and discuss any monuments or memorials that exist in your community.

national holiday | memorial | hero | veteran
independence | honor | monument | religious holiday

C. Use a word from above to finish each sentence.

1. Easter is a <u>religious holiday</u>.
2. On the Fourth of July, Americans celebrate their <u>independence</u>.
3. The Lincoln School was named as a <u>memorial</u> to President Abraham Lincoln.
4. The center of town has a <u>monument</u> of a war hero riding a horse.
5. Labor Day is a <u>national holiday</u> the whole country celebrates.
6. Grandpa is a <u>veteran</u> of a war.
7. You are a <u>hero</u> for saving people during the fire.
8. A parade is one way to <u>honor</u> people who have died in wars.

74 Heroes and Holidays

national holiday | memorial | hero | veteran
independence | honor | monument | religious holiday

Write!

What is your favorite holiday? Is it a religious holiday or a national holiday? Tell what you do to celebrate the holiday.

Answers will vary. See sample answer.

Heroes and Holidays 75

Write!

Have students work with a partner to brainstorm ideas for writing. Then provide each student with a copy of Writing Graphic Organizer: Web, Teacher Guide page 71, to use before they start writing. In the center circle, students should write the name of their favorite holiday. In the other circles, they should write details about that event. Provide students with a sentence starter such as, *My favorite holiday is* ________. Guide them to tell if the holiday is religious or national, and then tell how they celebrate it.

Sample Answer

My favorite holiday is Thanksgiving. It is a national holiday. My family eats special foods. We eat turkey and stuffing. We eat apple pie. Before we eat, we tell why we are thankful.

TAKE-HOME ACTIVITY

Assign the Take-Home Activity to students for additional practice with the target vocabulary words. The reproducible Take-Home Activity for Lesson 12 is on page 84 of the Teacher Guide.

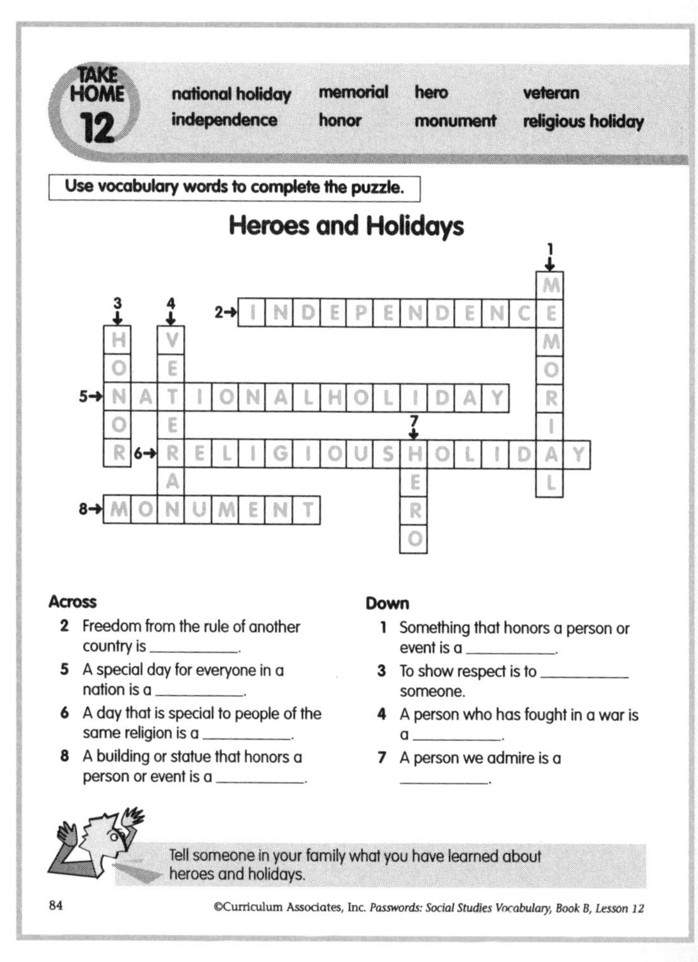

TAKE HOME 12

national holiday | memorial | hero | veteran
independence | honor | monument | religious holiday

Use vocabulary words to complete the puzzle.

Heroes and Holidays

Across

2 Freedom from the rule of another country is ________.

5 A special day for everyone in a nation is a ________.

6 A day that is special to people of the same religion is a ________.

8 A building or statue that honors a person or event is a ________.

Down

1 Something that honors a person or event is a ________.

3 To show respect is to ________ someone.

4 A person who has fought in a war is a ________.

7 A person we admire is a ________.

Tell someone in your family what you have learned about heroes and holidays.

84

Name ______________________________ Date ______________

Vocabulary Graphic Organizer: Four Square

Draw a picture.	Use the word in a sentence.
Word	
Definition	Examples

Name ______________________ Date ______________

Vocabulary Graphic Organizer: Word Web

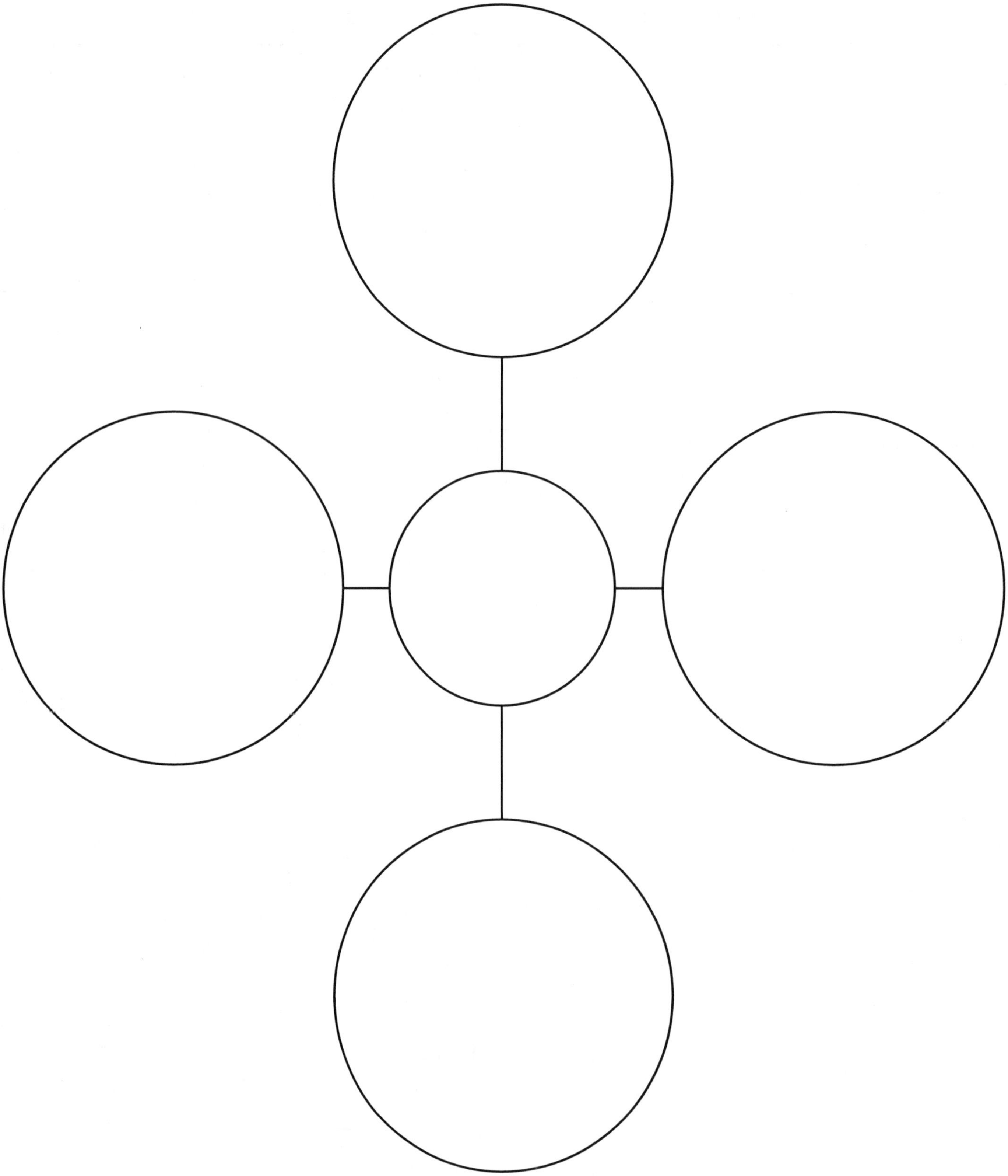

Name ______________________________ Date ______________

Vocabulary Graphic Organizer: Knowledge Scale

Vocabulary Word	Don't Know It	Not Sure	Know It	Definition

Name ______________________________ Date ______________

Writing Graphic Organizer: Main Idea and Details Chart

Main Idea	Details
1.	
2.	

Name ______________________________ Date ______________

Writing Graphic Organizer: Web

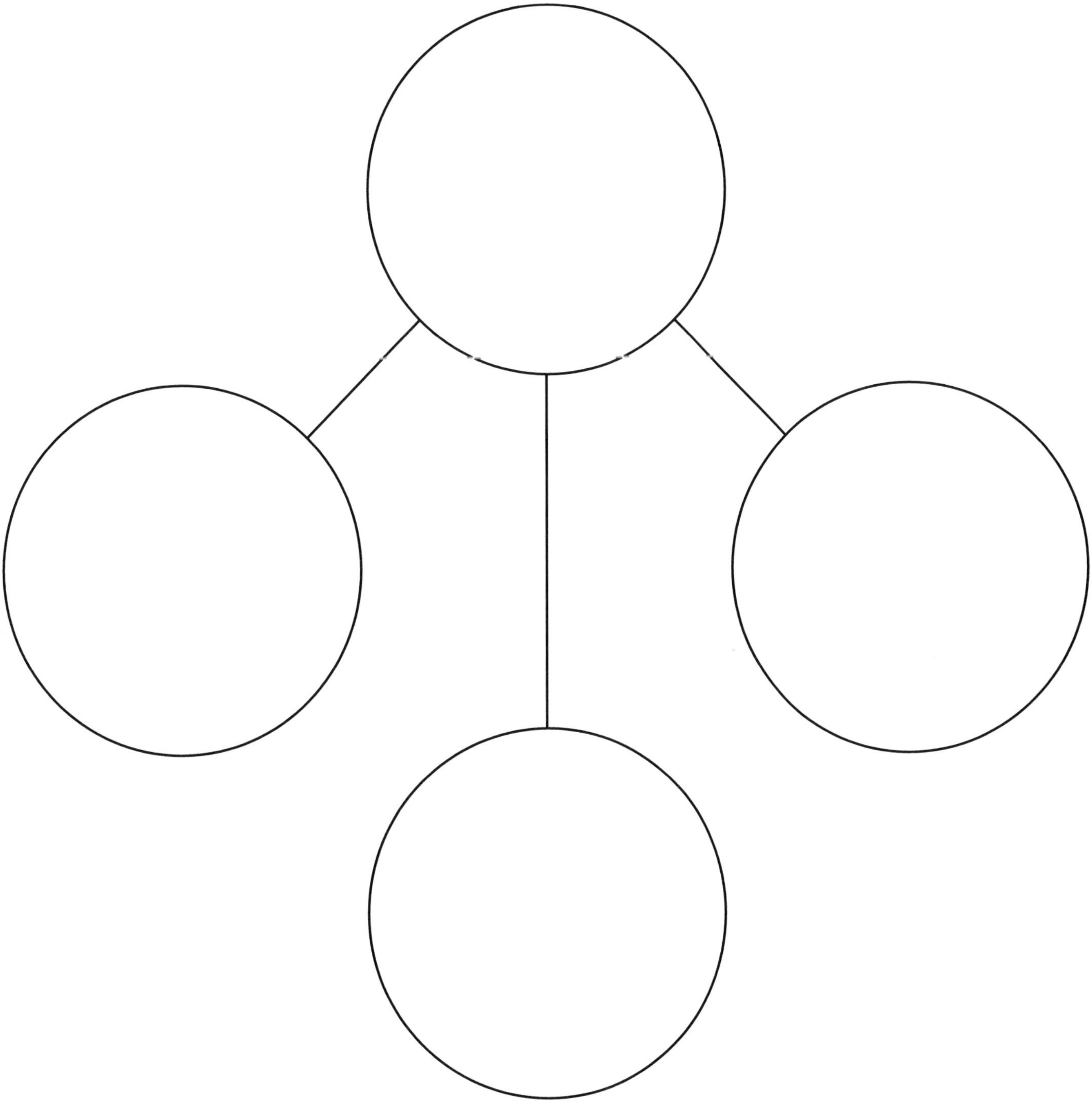

Name ______________________________ Date ______________

Writing Graphic Organizer: Details Cube

LESSON 1

geography	mountain	island	lake
landform	valley	ocean	river

Use vocabulary words to complete the puzzle.

Land and Water

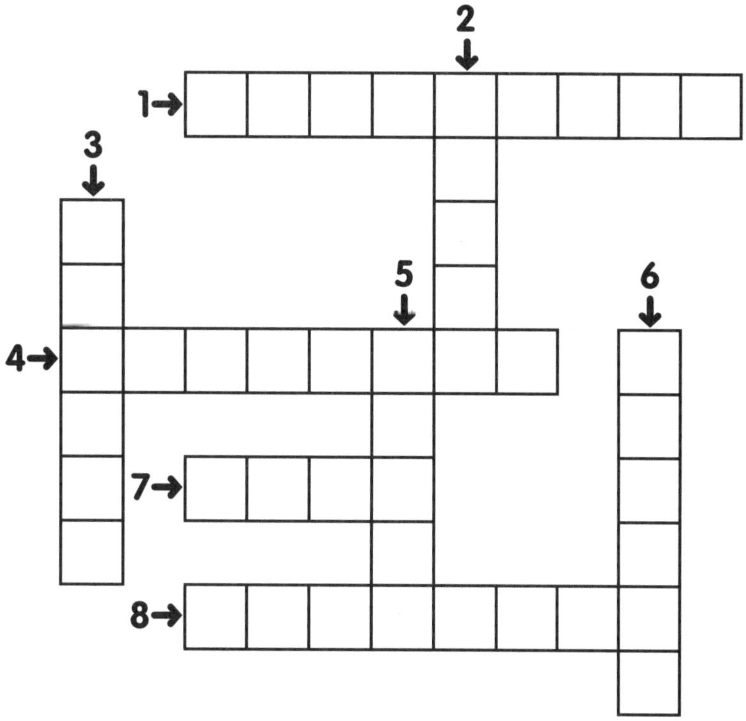

ACROSS

1 The study of the Earth's land and water is called ___________.

4 Any kind of land with any shape is a ___________.

7 Water with land all around it is a ___________.

8 The highest kind of land is a ___________.

DOWN

2 Water that flows across land is a ___________.

3 The low land between mountains is called a ___________.

5 A very large body of water is an ___________.

6 Land that has water all around it is an ___________.

Tell someone in your family what you have learned about land and water.

community | neighborhood | rural area | country
urban area | suburb | continent | state

Use vocabulary words to complete the puzzle.

Communities Are Different

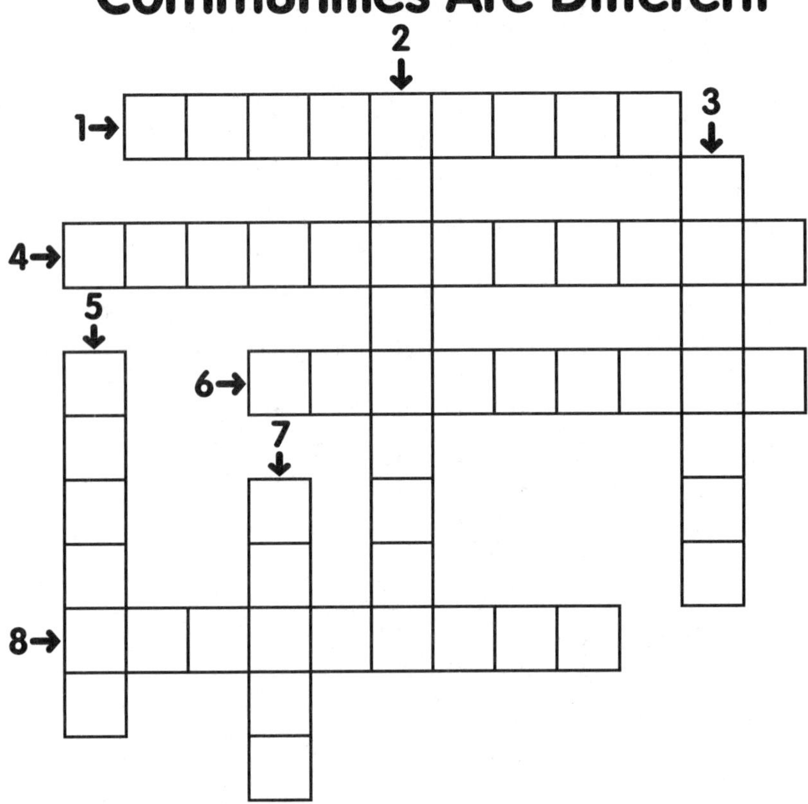

ACROSS

1 A place where people live is a ____________.

4 A part of a city or town is a ____________.

6 A large body of land is a ____________.

8 A place that has fewer stores or houses than a city or town is a ____________.

DOWN

2 Another name for a city is an ____________.

3 A land with the same laws is called a ____________.

5 A town near a city is sometimes called a ____________.

7 One part of a country is called a ____________.

Tell someone in your family what you have learned about how communities are different.

weather · season · desert · environment
climate · region · natural resources · recycle

Use vocabulary words to complete the puzzle.

People and the Environment

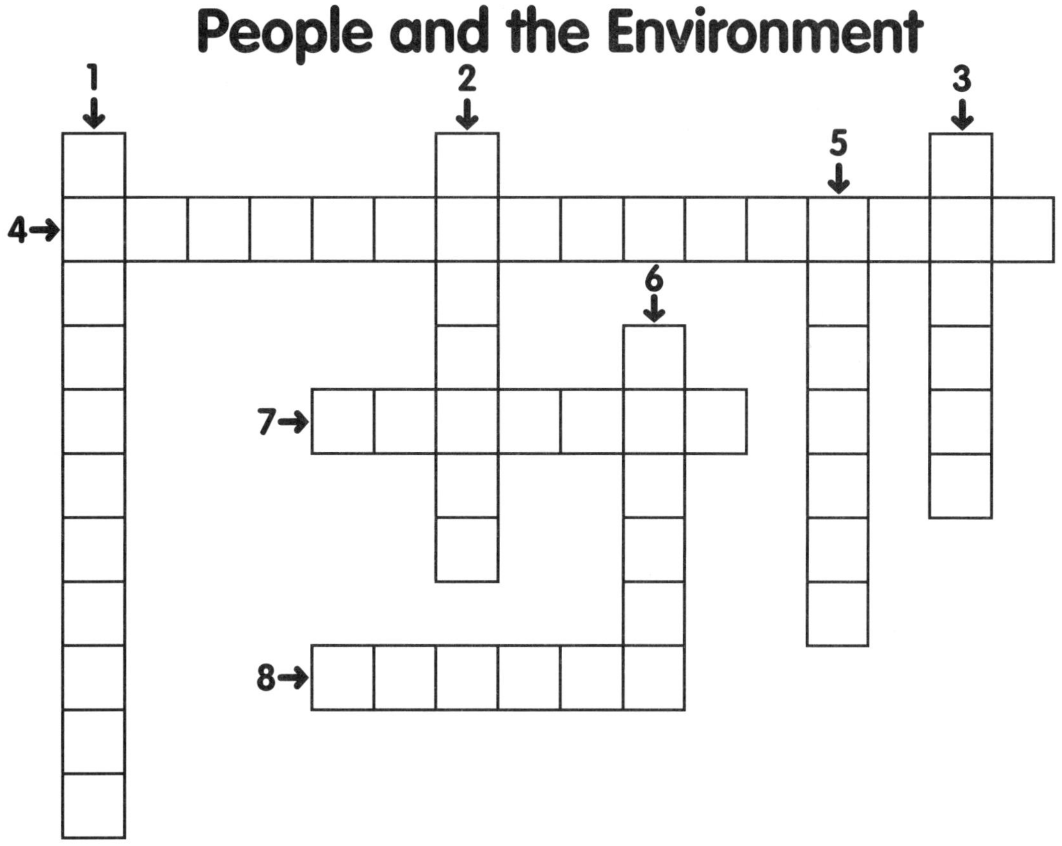

ACROSS

4 The things in nature that people use are called ____________.

7 What the air is like outside is the ____________.

8 An area that shares some features is a ____________.

DOWN

1 The natural world around you is the ____________.

2 The usual weather of a place over a long time is called the ____________.

3 A region that gets very little rain is called a ____________.

5 One way to use resources wisely is to ____________ .

6 A time of the year is a ____________.

Tell someone in your family what you have learned about people and the environment.

citizen	citizenship	vote	law
right	responsibility	rule	judge

Use vocabulary words to complete the puzzle.

Good Citizens

ACROSS

4 A person who decides the best way to follow the laws is a ___________.

6 A person who belongs to a place is a ___________.

7 You show what you are for or against when you ___________.

8 A rule that everyone must follow is a ___________.

DOWN

1 Good behavior as a citizen is called ___________.

2 Something that tells people what they should or should not do is a ___________.

3 Something you should do is a ___________.

5 Something you are free to do is a ___________.

1↓ 2↓ 3↓ 4→ 5↓ 6→ 7→ 8→

Tell someone in your family what you have learned about good citizens.

TAKE HOME 5

government	leader	mayor	governor
local government	election	city council	tax

Use vocabulary words to complete the puzzle.

Government

ACROSS

3 The special time when we vote for our leaders is called an ____________.

4 The people who run a city or a town are the ____________.

6 People who run the community, state, or country are the ____________.

8 People who help a mayor run a town are members of the ____________.

DOWN

1 A state's leader is the ____________.

2 A person who leads others is a ____________.

5 Money from citizens and businesses is called a ____________.

7 A town's leader is a ____________.

Tell someone in your family what you have learned about government.

nation | Congress | president | Supreme Court
branches | Capitol | White House | Constitution

Use vocabulary words to complete the puzzle.

Our Nation's Government

1↓ 2→ 3↓ 4↓ 5↓ 6→ 7→ 8→

ACROSS

2 The leader of our nation is the ____________.

6 Another word for country is ____________.

7 The law of the land is the ____________.

8 The highest court in the nation is the ____________.

DOWN

1 The President lives in the ____________.

3 The part of the government that makes the laws is ____________.

4 Our national government is made of three parts, or ____________.

5 The people in Congress work in a building called the ____________.

Tell someone in your family what you have learned about our nation's government.

goods	price	wants	services
market	needs	income	savings account

Use vocabulary words to complete the puzzle.

Work and Money

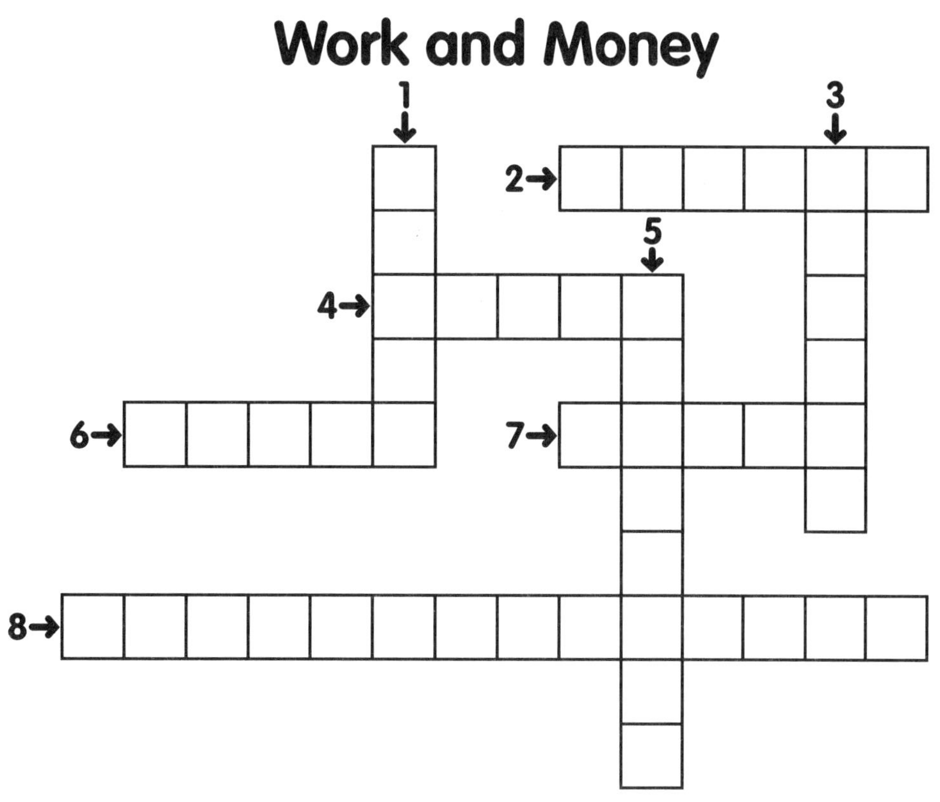

ACROSS

2 The money a person gets from working is called ____________.

4 Things that people must have to live are called ____________.

6 Things that are made or grown are called ____________.

7 The amount of money you pay to buy something is its ____________.

8 A bank service that lets people keep their money safe is a ____________.

DOWN

1 Things that people would like to have are called ____________.

3 A place to buy and sell things is a ____________.

5 Jobs people do to help others are called ____________.

Tell someone in your family what you have learned about work and money.

producers	trade	factory	specialize
consumers	barter	scarcity	technology

Use vocabulary words to complete the puzzle.

Producing Goods

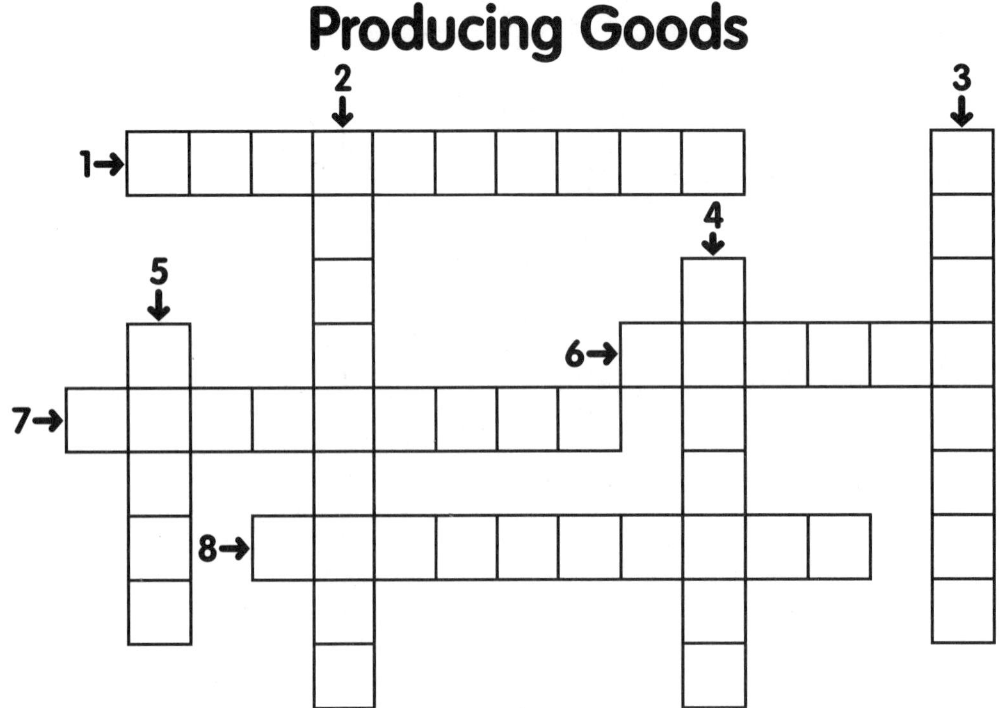

ACROSS

1 To grow or make just one product is to ____________.

6 Trading goods without money is called ____________.

7 People who make or grow goods to sell are ____________.

8 The use of science to make new things is ____________.

DOWN

2 The people who buy goods are ____________.

3 Not enough shoes were made so now there is a ____________.

4 A place where goods are made is a ____________.

5 The buying and selling of services is called ____________.

Tell someone in your family what you have learned about producing goods.

history	pioneer	transportation	communication
wilderness	settlement	steamboat	skyscraper

Use vocabulary words to complete the puzzle.

Communities Change

ACROSS

2 A large, natural place is a ____________.

6 What we know about the past is called ____________.

7 A boat that gets power from boiling water is a ____________.

8 One of the first people to live in a place is a ____________.

DOWN

1 A small, new town is a ____________.

3 Sharing information is called ____________.

4 A way of moving things or people from one place to another is ____________.

5 A very tall building is a ____________.

Tell someone in your family what you have learned about how communities change.

culture custom tradition legend
belief celebrate ceremony storyteller

Use vocabulary words to complete the puzzle.

Communities Near and Far

Across

3 Something that people usually do at a certain time is a ____________.

5 Something we think is true is a ____________.

7 A special activity that we do at a certain time is a ____________.

8 Something people do the same way year after year is a ____________.

Down

1 A person who tells a story is a ____________.

2 A way of life for a group of people is a ____________.

4 To honor a special day by doing something special is to ____________.

6 A story about things that happened long ago is a ____________.

Tell someone in your family what you have learned about communities near and far.

symbol liberty landmark immigrant ancestor journey courage language

Use vocabulary words to complete the puzzle.

Americans Come from Many Places

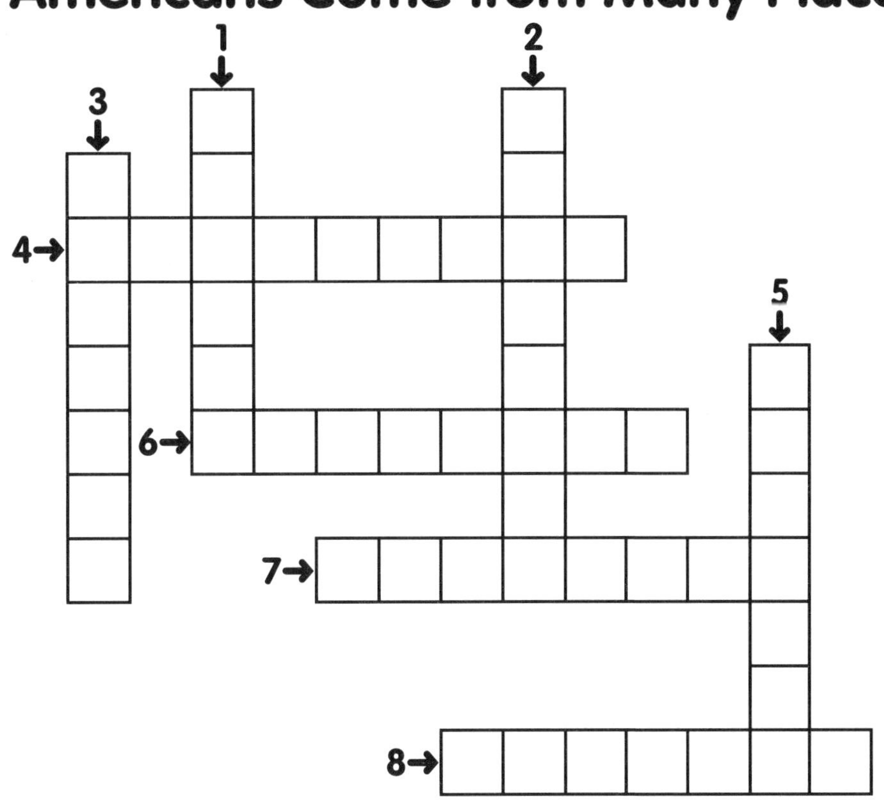

Across

4 A person who moves from one country to another is an ___________.

6 Something that helps people know a place is a ___________.

7 A family member who lived before you is your ___________.

8 A long trip is a ___________.

Down

1 Something that stands for something else is a ___________.

2 The set of words people use to speak to each other is their ___________.

3 Another word for freedom is ___________.

5 Something you show when you do something scary is ___________.

Tell someone in your family what you have learned about how Americans come from many places.

national holiday | memorial | hero | veteran
independence | honor | monument | religious holiday

Use vocabulary words to complete the puzzle.

Heroes and Holidays

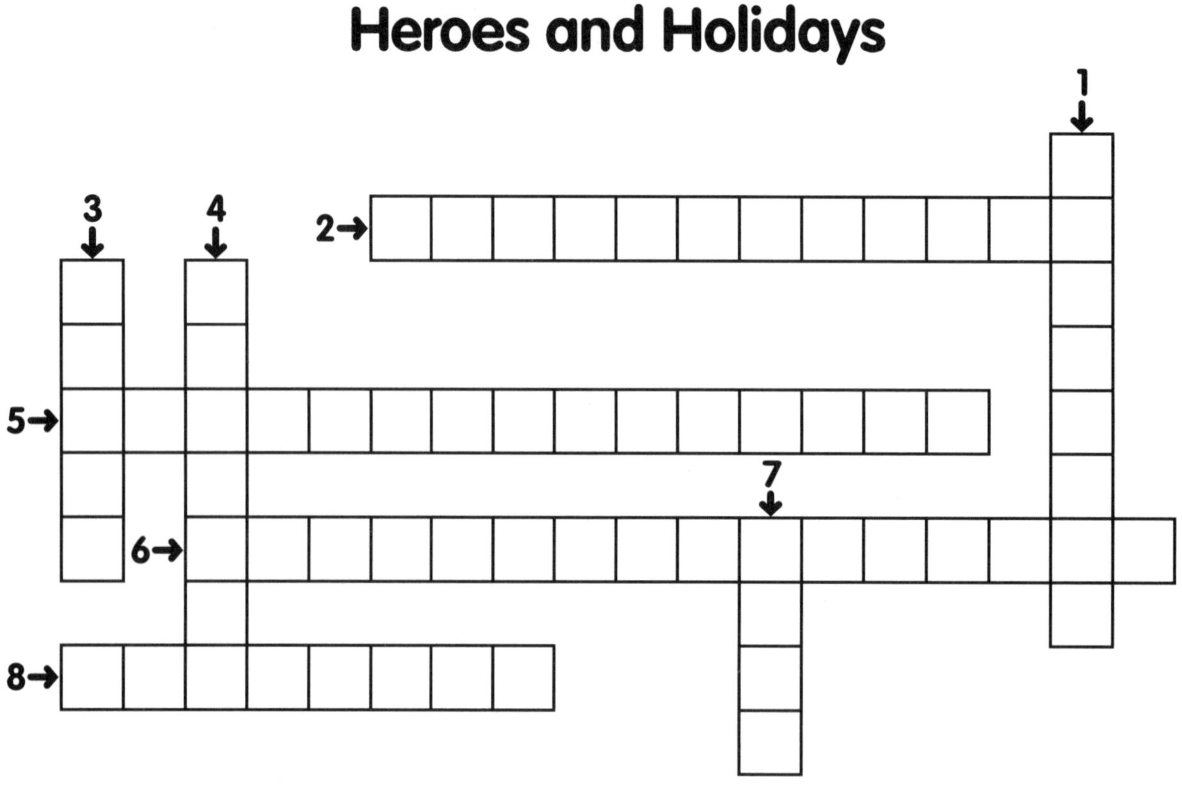

Across

2 Freedom from the rule of another country is ____________.

5 A special day for everyone in a nation is a ____________.

6 A day that is special to people of the same religion is a ____________.

8 A building or statue that honors a person or event is a ____________.

Down

1 Something that honors a person or event is a ____________.

3 To show respect is to ____________ someone.

4 A person who has fought in a war is a ____________.

7 A person we admire is a ____________.

Tell someone in your family what you have learned about heroes and holidays.

geography

island

landform

ocean

mountain

lake

valley

river

land that has water all around it

the study of Earth's land and water

a very large body of water

any kind of land with a shape

water with land all around it

the highest kind of land

water that flows across land

the low land between mountains

community

rural area

urban area

continent

neighborhood

country

suburb

state

a place that has fewer stores or houses than a city or town

a place where people live

a large body of land

another name for a city

a land with the same laws

a part of a city or town

one part of a country

a town near a city

weather

desert

climate

natural resources

season

environment

region

recycle

a dry region where there is little rain

what the air is like outside

the things in nature that people use

the usual weather of a place over a long time

the natural world around you

a time of year

changing something so it can be used again

an area that shares some features

citizen

vote

right

rule

citizenship

law

responsibility

judge

to show what you are for or against

a person who belongs to a place

something that tells people what they should or should not do

something you are free to do

a rule that everyone must follow

good behavior as a citizen

a person who decides the best way to follow the laws

something you should do

government

mayor

local government

city council

leader

governor

election

tax

the leader of a town or a city

the people who work together to run a city or town, state, or country

the people who help the mayor run a town

the people who work together to run a town or a city

the leader of a state

a person who leads others

money from people and businesses that helps pay for the needs of the community

a special time when we vote for our leaders

nation

president

branches

White House

Congress

Supreme Court

Capitol

Constitution

the leader of our nation

another word for country

the house where the president lives

the parts of the government

the highest court in the nation

the part of government that makes the laws

the law of the land

the building where Congress works

goods

wants

market

income

price

services

needs

savings account

things that people would like to have

things that are made or grown

the money that a person gets from working

a place to buy and sell things

jobs people do to help other people

the amount of money you pay to buy something

a bank service that lets people keep their money safe

things that people must have to live

producers

factory

consumers

scarcity

trade

specialize

barter

technology

a place where goods are made

the people who make or grow goods to sell

when there is not enough of something

the people who buy goods

to grow or make just one product

the buying and selling of goods and services

the use of science to make new things

the trading of goods or services without using money

history

transportation

wilderness

steamboat

pioneer

communication

settlement

skyscraper

a way of moving things or people from one place to another

what we know about the past

a boat that gets power from boiling water

a large, natural place without towns or people

the sharing of news and ideas

one of the first people to live in a place

a very tall building

a small, new town

culture

tradition

belief

ceremony

custom

legend

celebrate

storyteller

something that people do the same way year after year

a way of life for a group of people

an event with special words and actions

something we think is true

a story that is passed on for many years

something that people usually do at a certain time

a person who tells stories

to honor a special day by doing something special

symbol

ancestor

liberty

journey

landmark

courage

immigrant

language

a family member who lived before you

something that stands for something else

a long trip

freedom

what people show when they do something even though they are afraid

something that helps people know a place

the set of words people use to speak to one another

a person who comes to a country to live

national holiday

hero

independence

monument

memorial

veteran

honor

religious holiday

someone who does brave or great things

a special day for everyone in a nation

a building or statue that honors a hero or event

freedom from the rule of another country

a person who has fought in a war

something that honors a person or event

a special day for people of the same religion

to do something to show that we think highly of someone

Notes

Notes

Notes

Notes